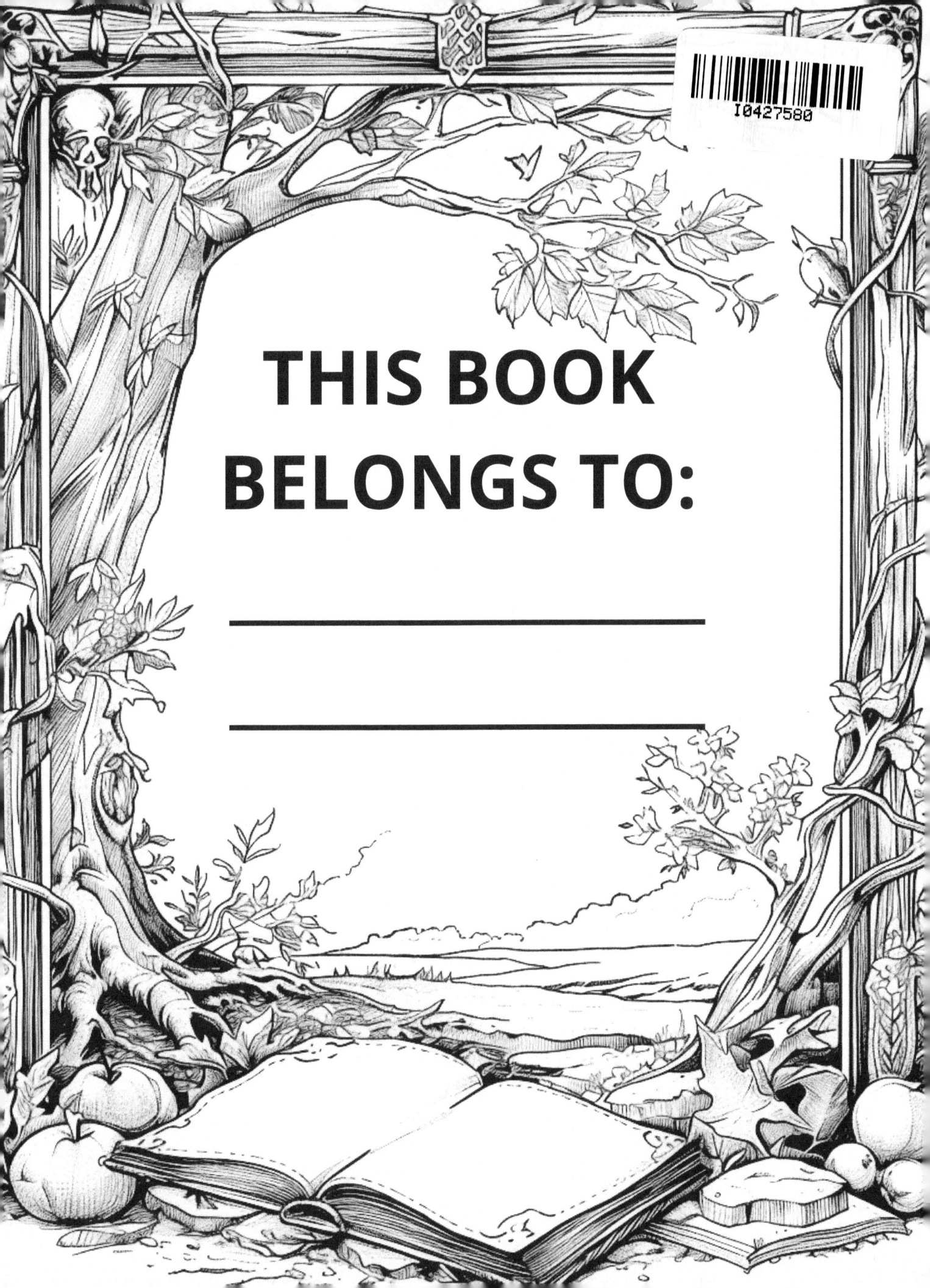

THIS BOOK BELONGS TO:

_____

_____

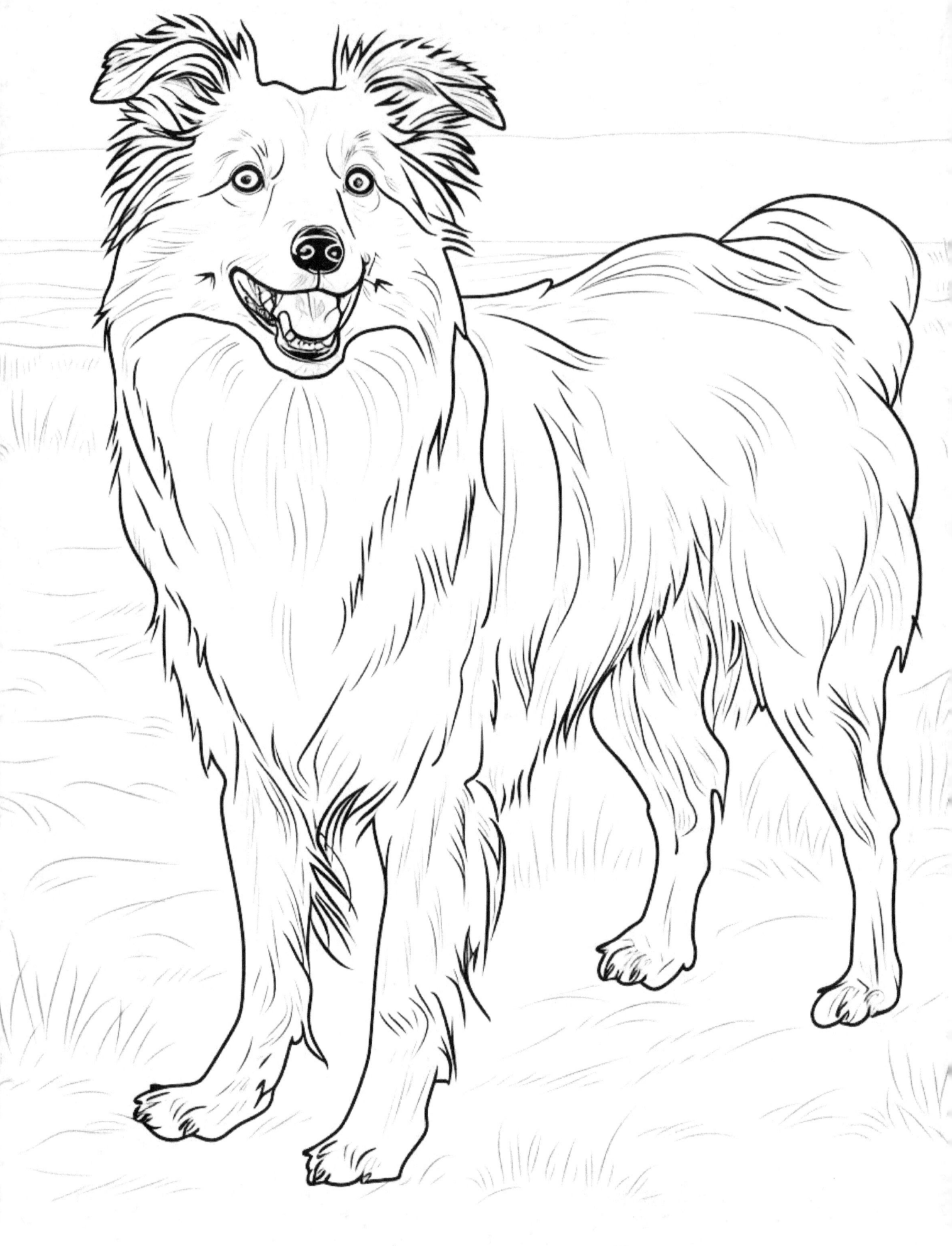

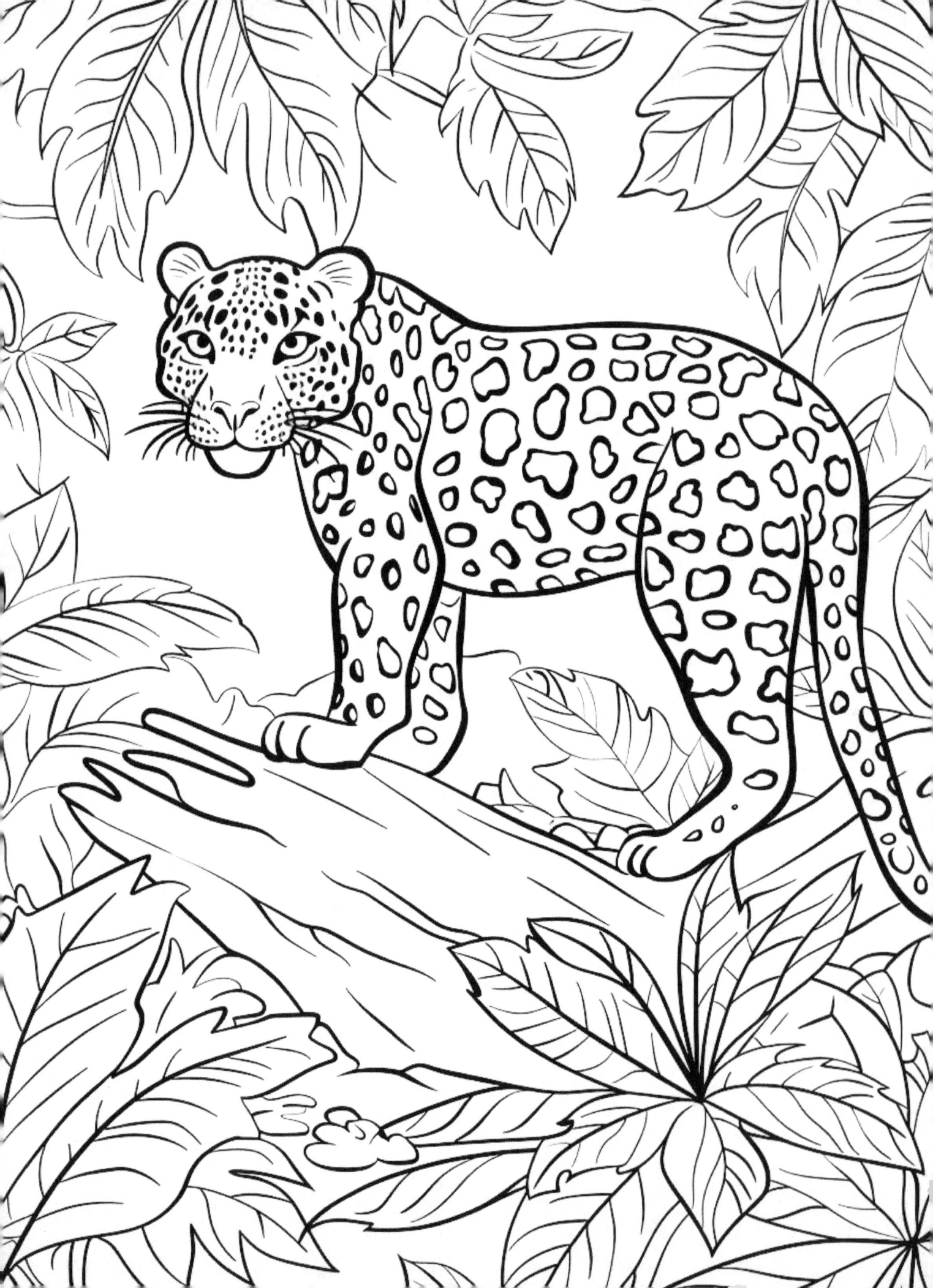

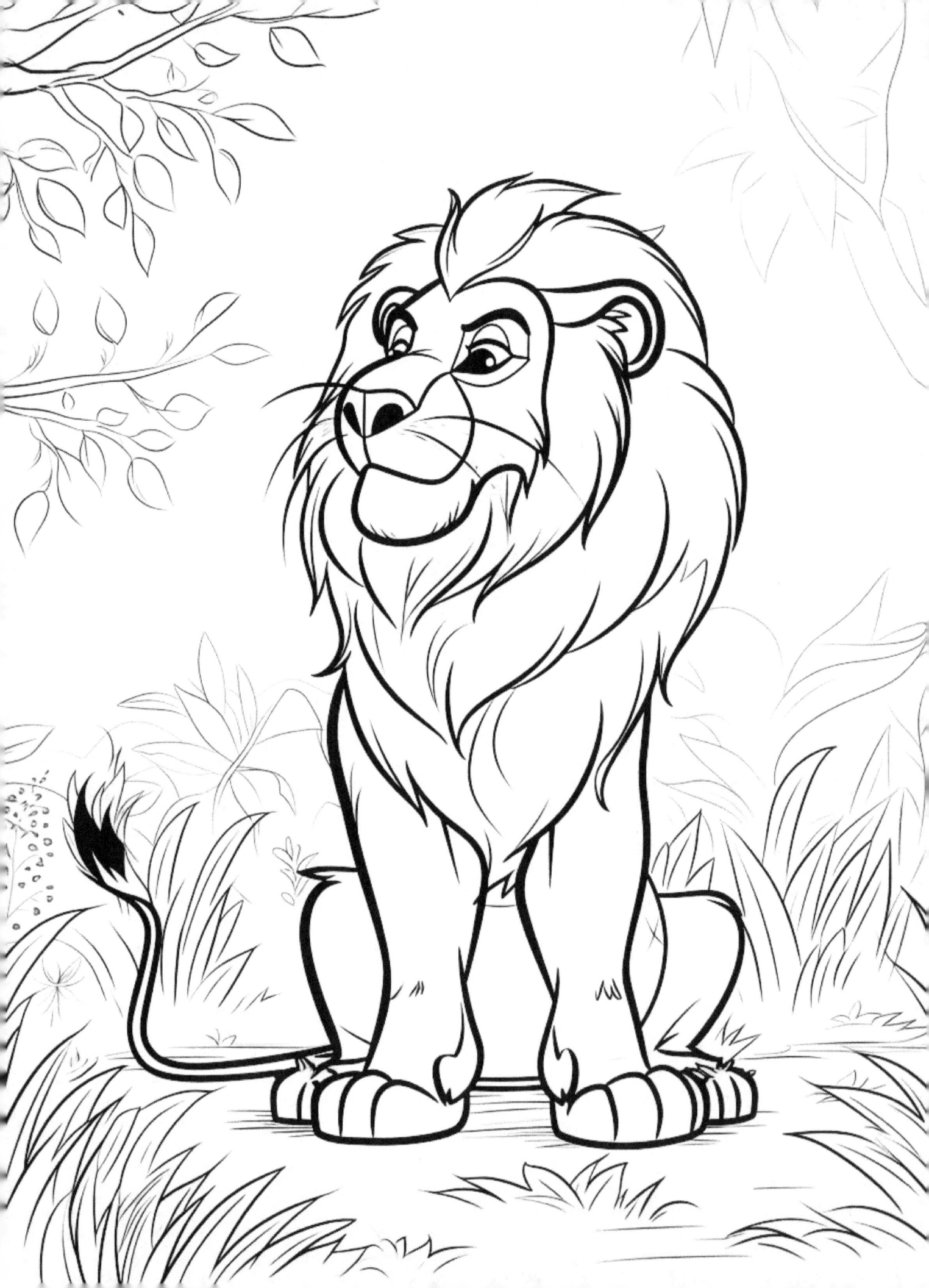

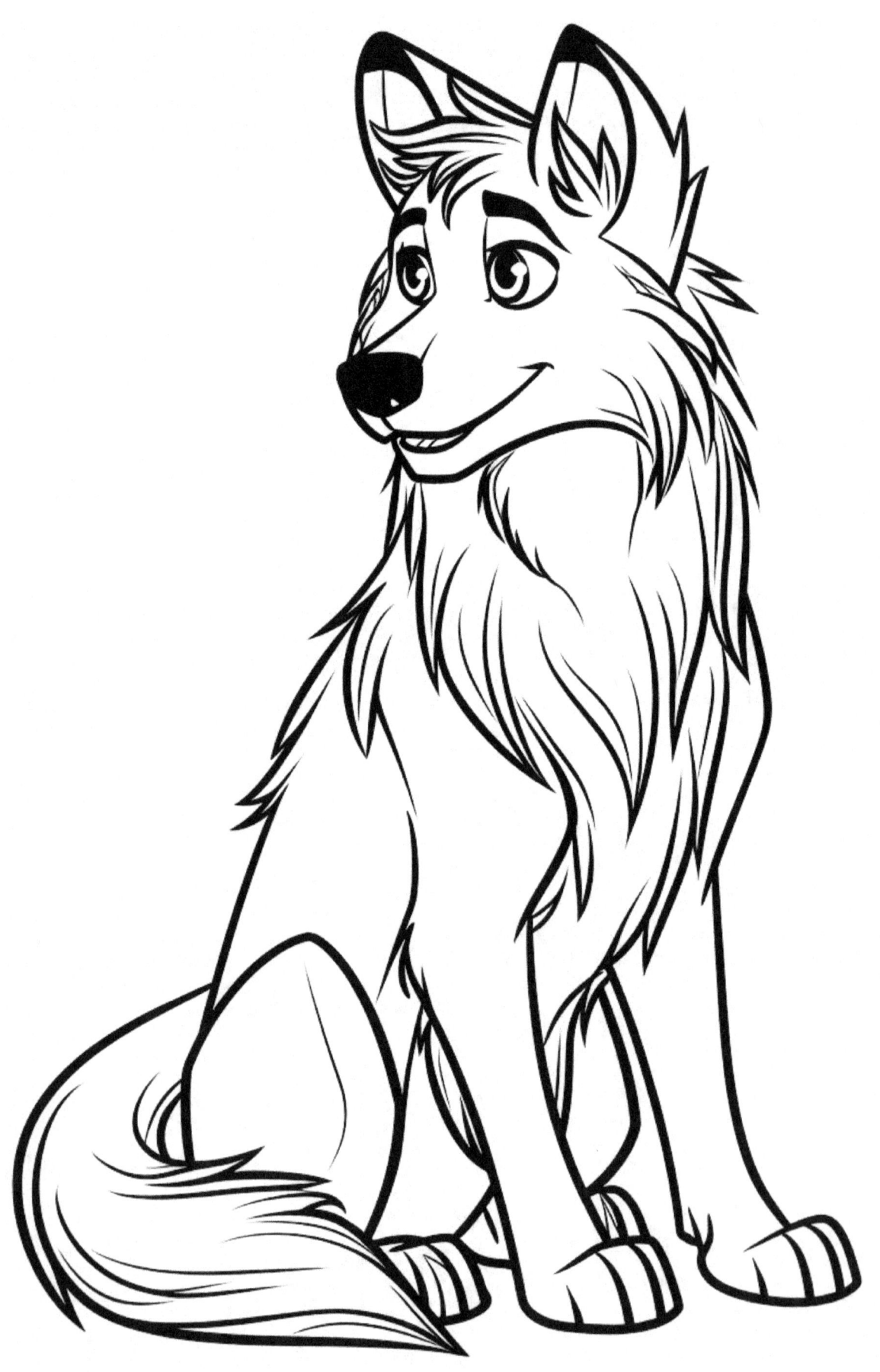

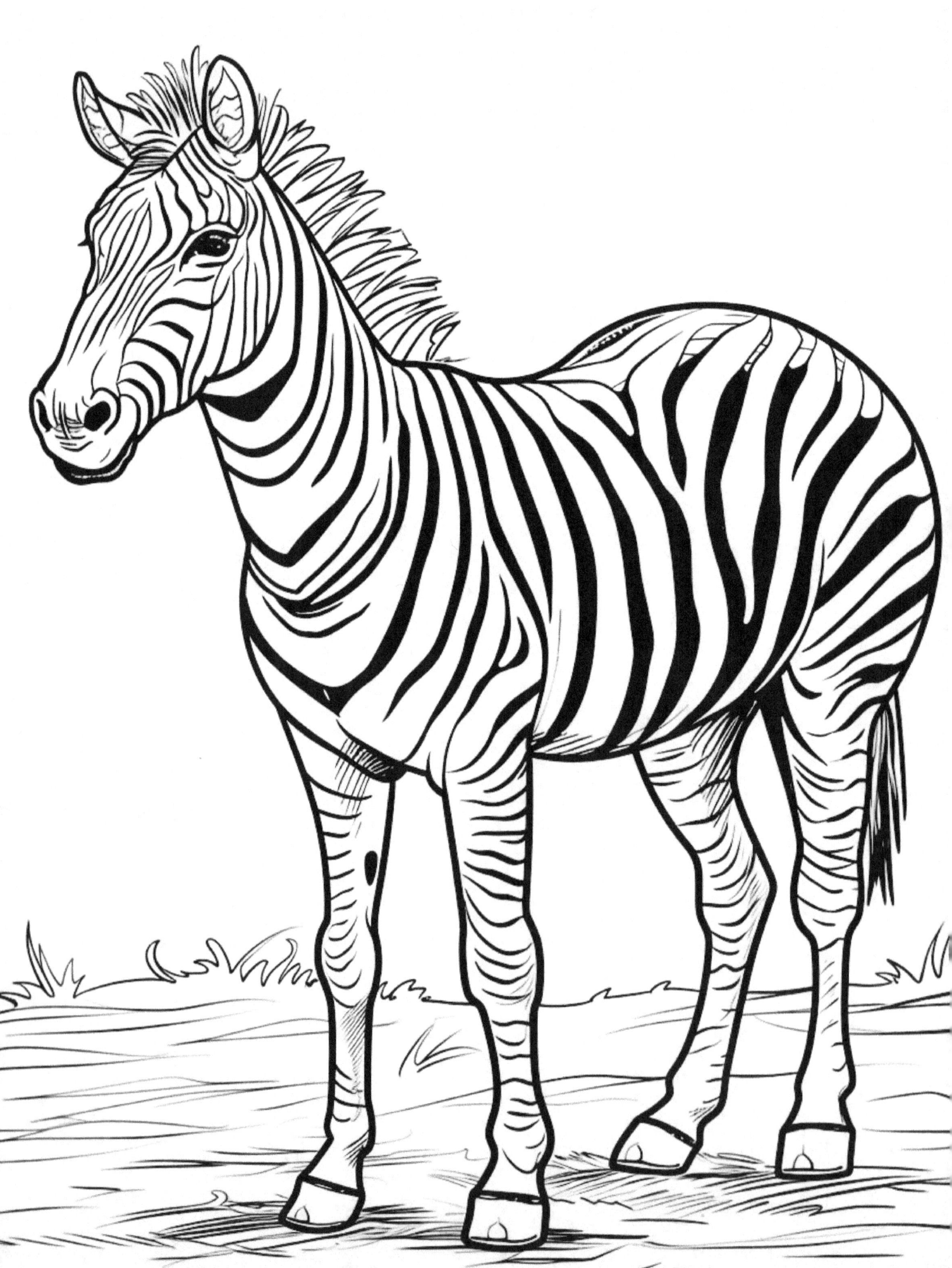

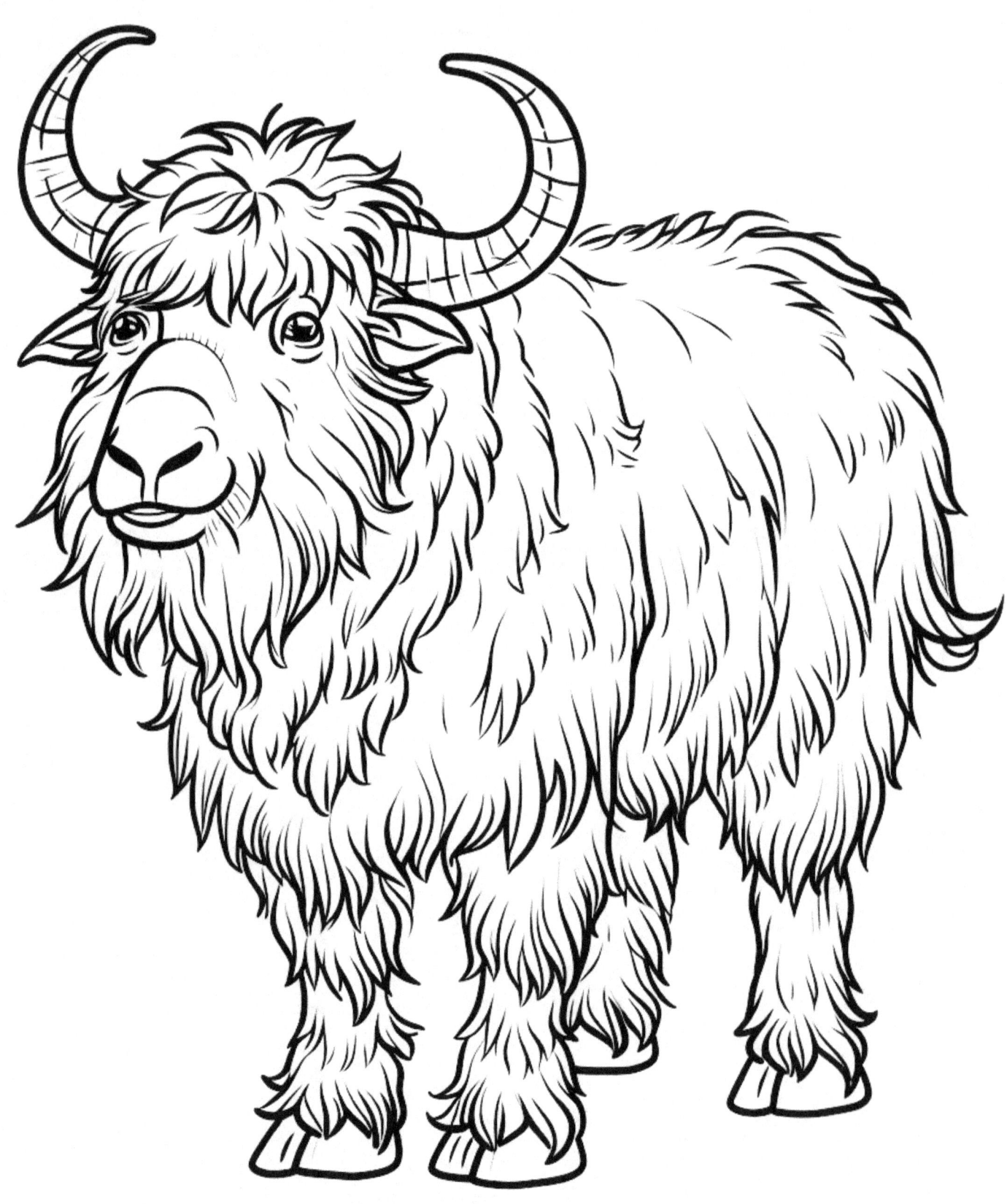

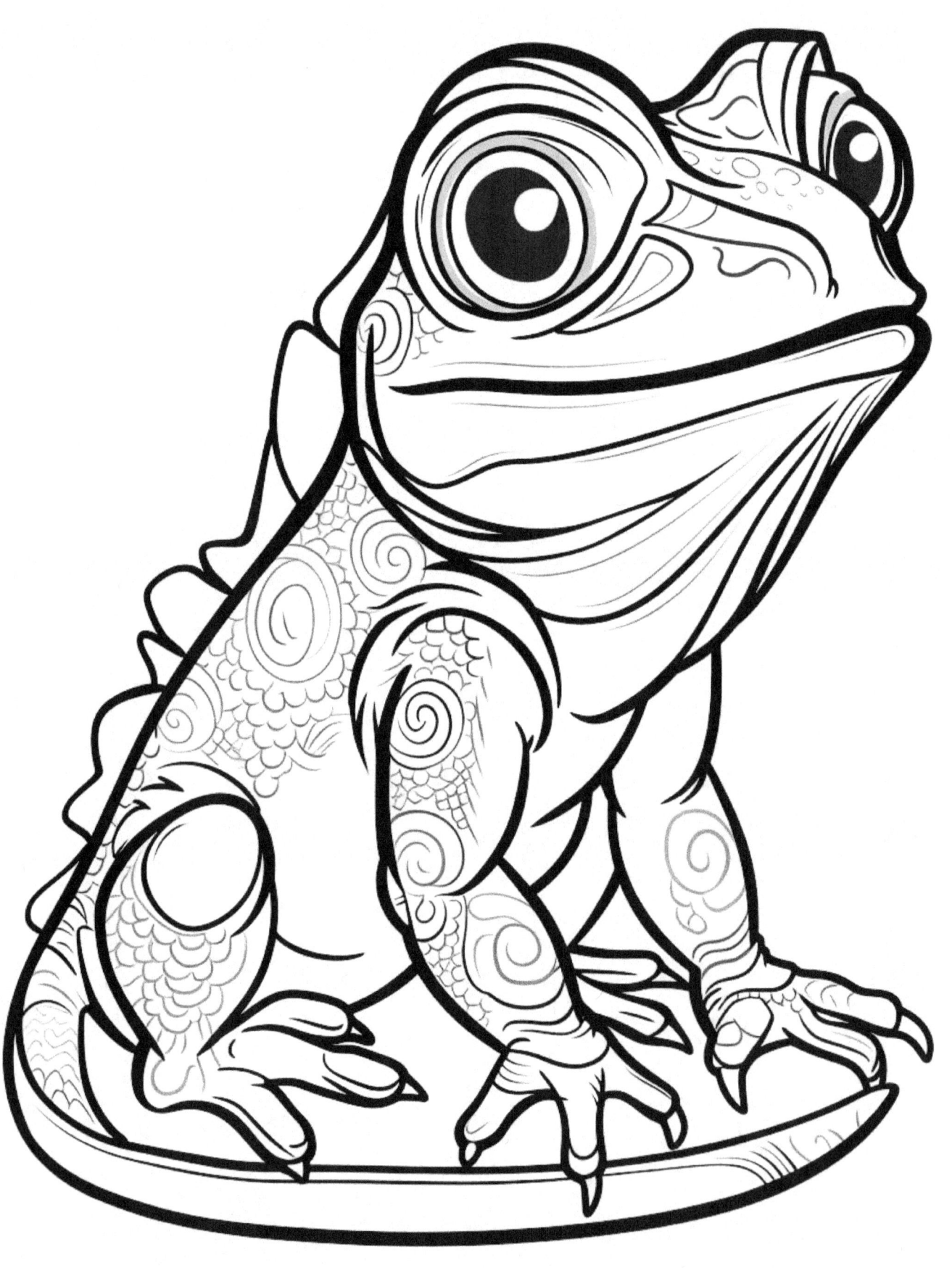

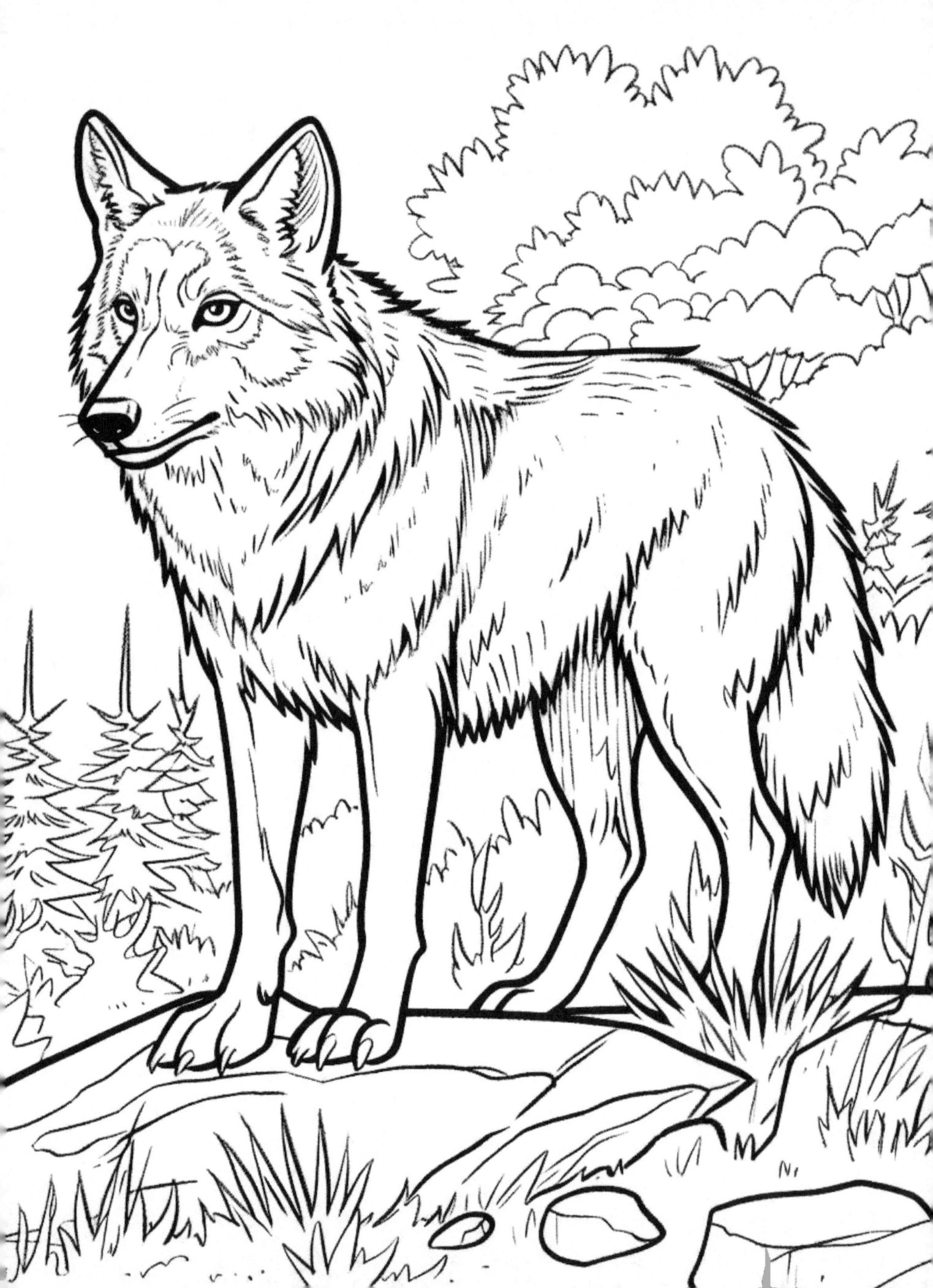

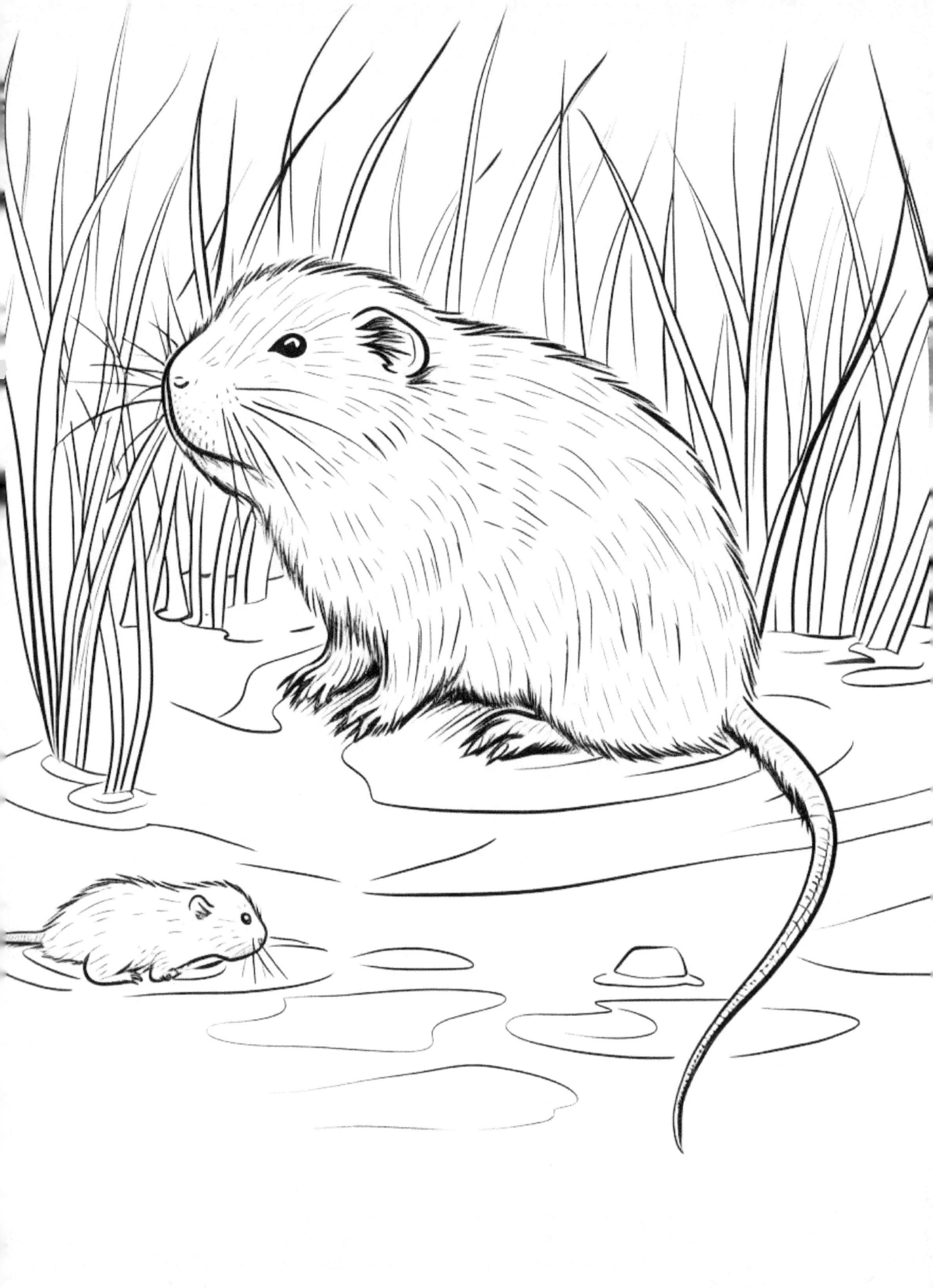

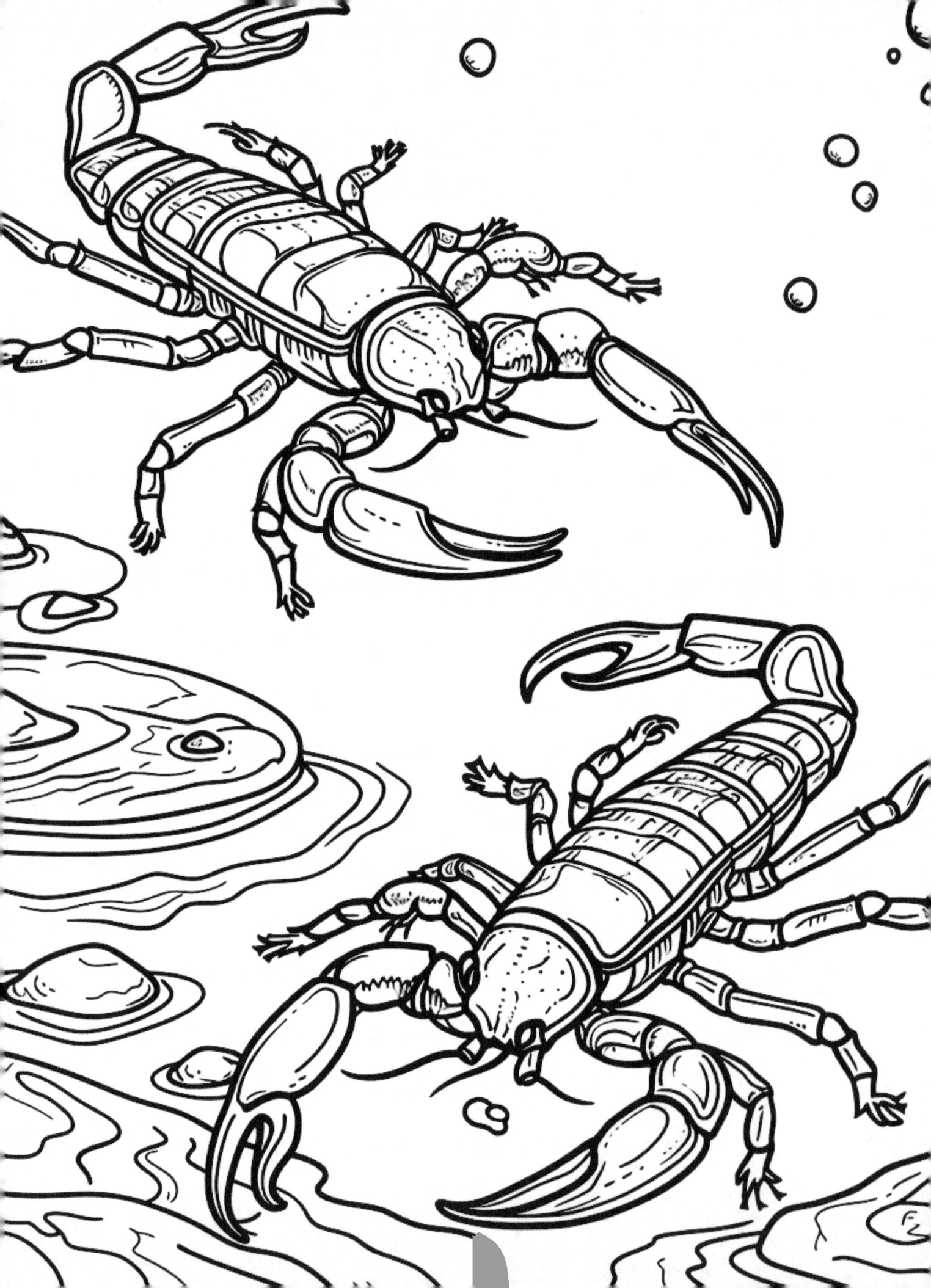

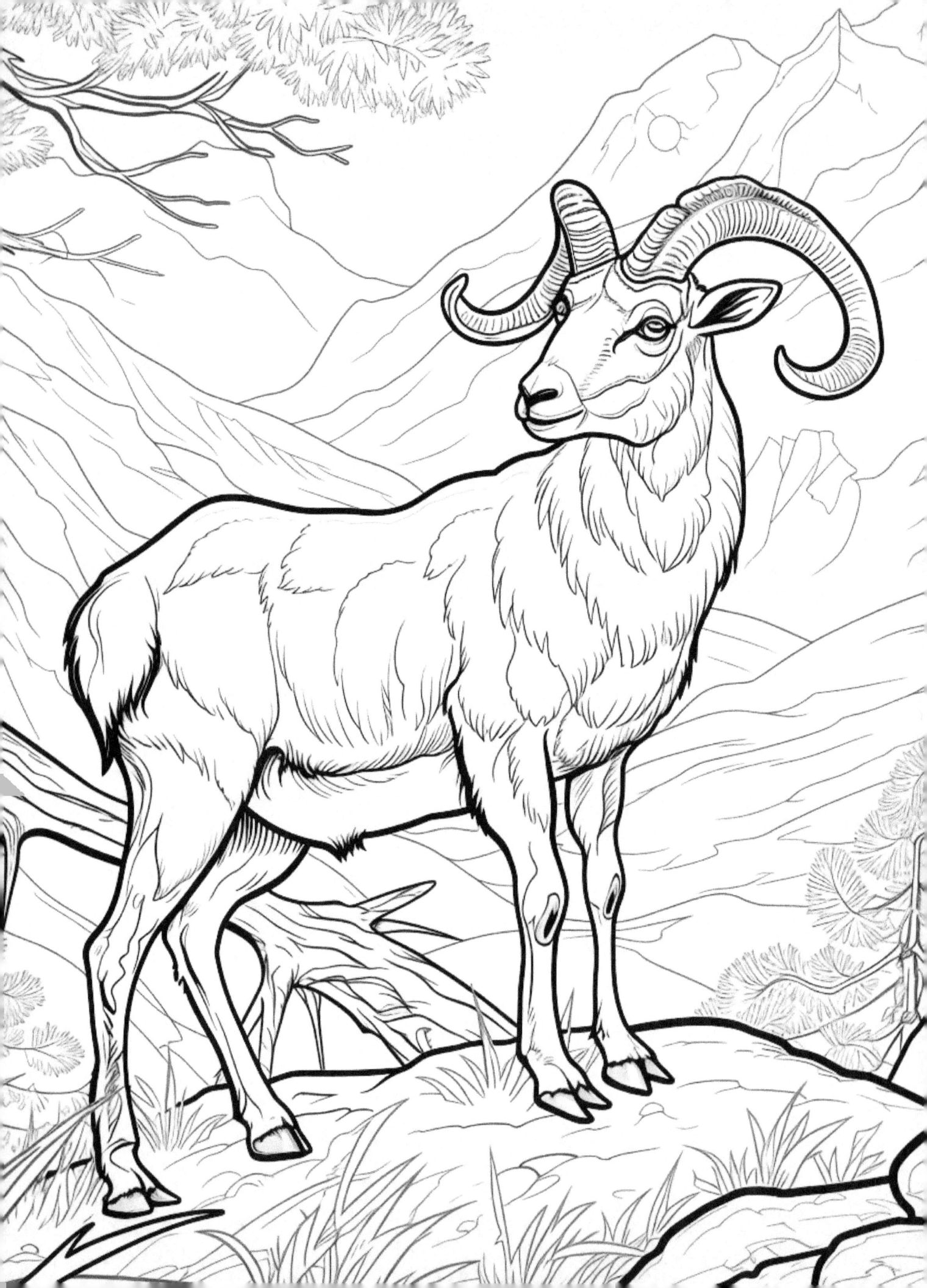

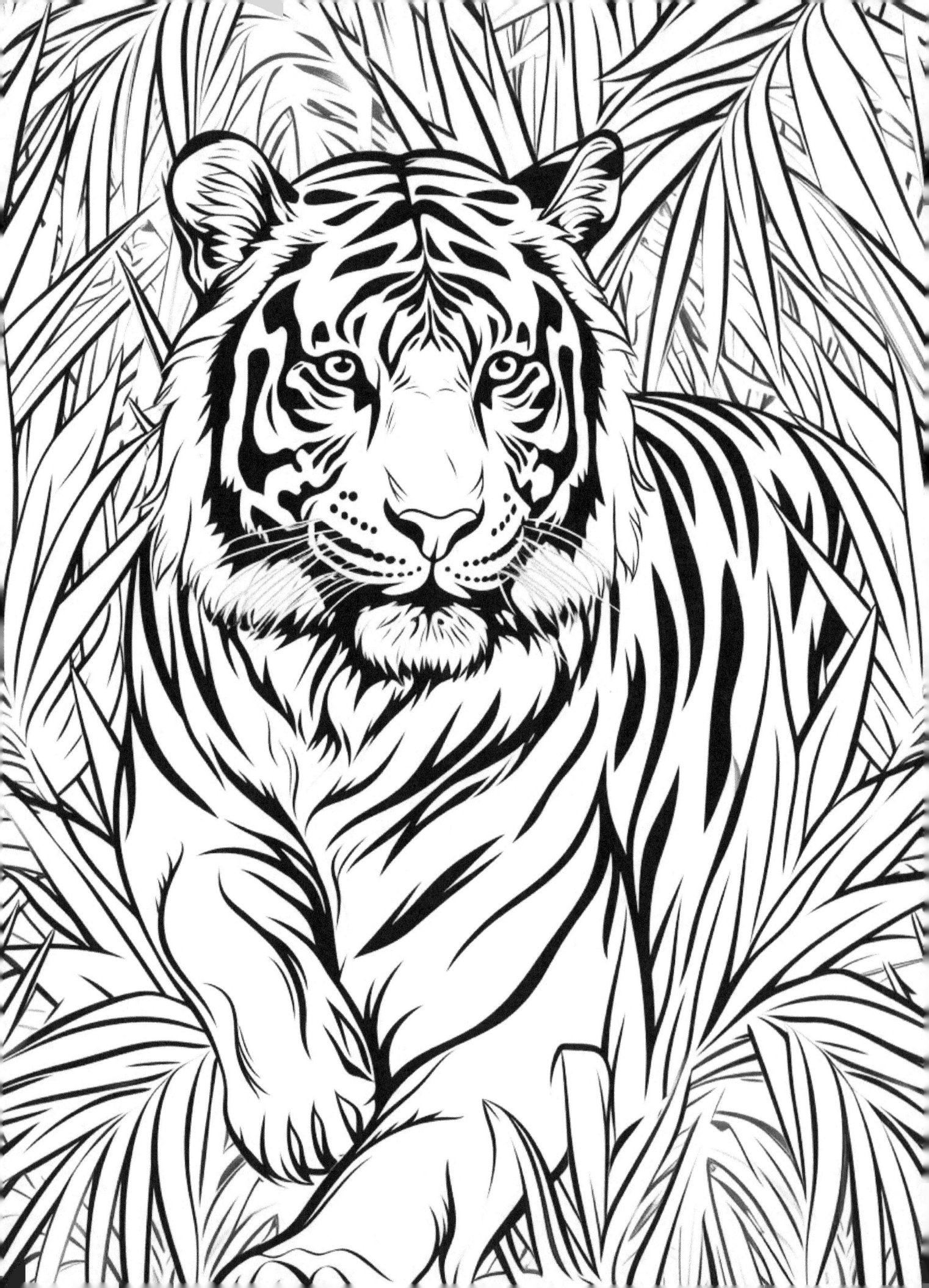

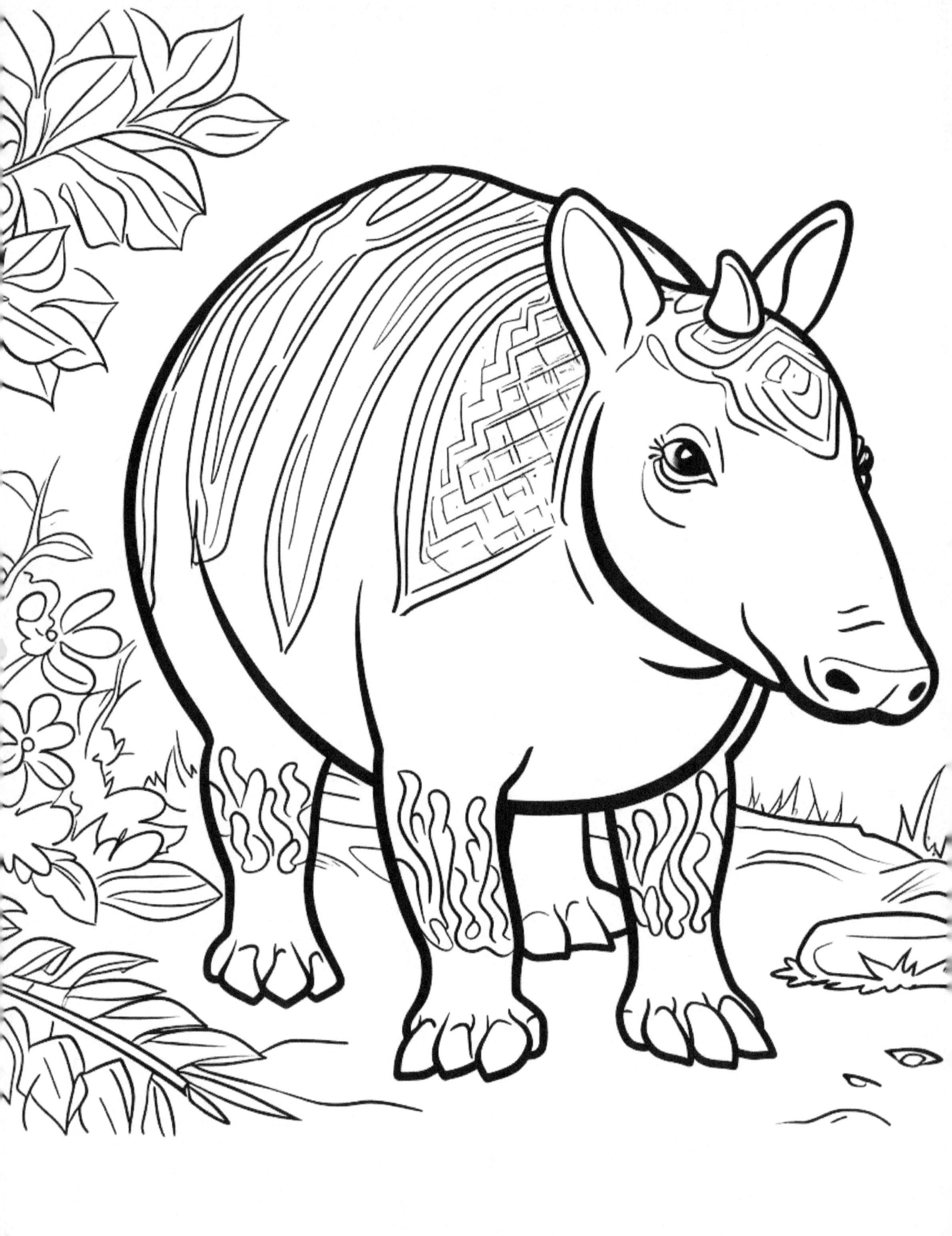

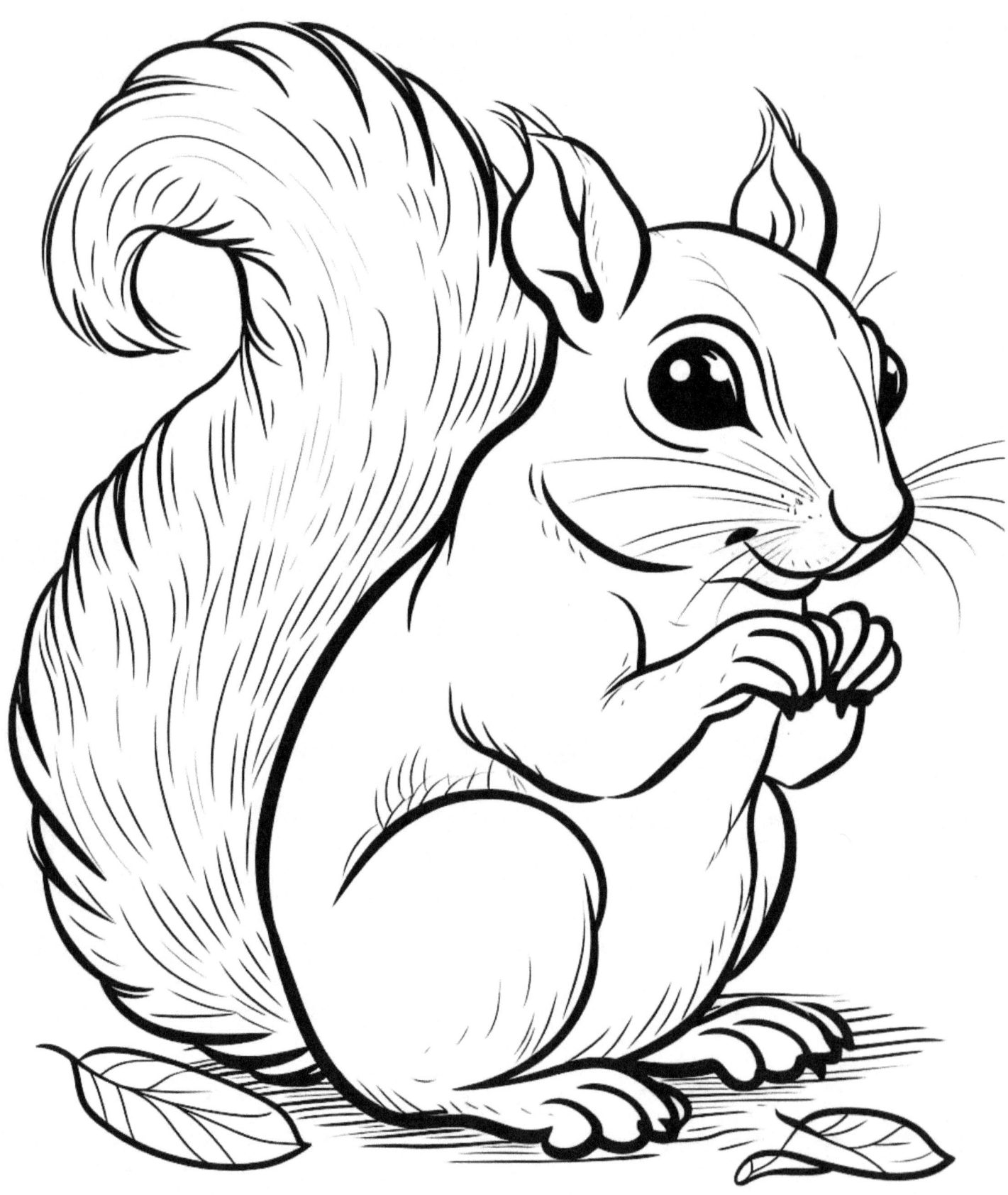

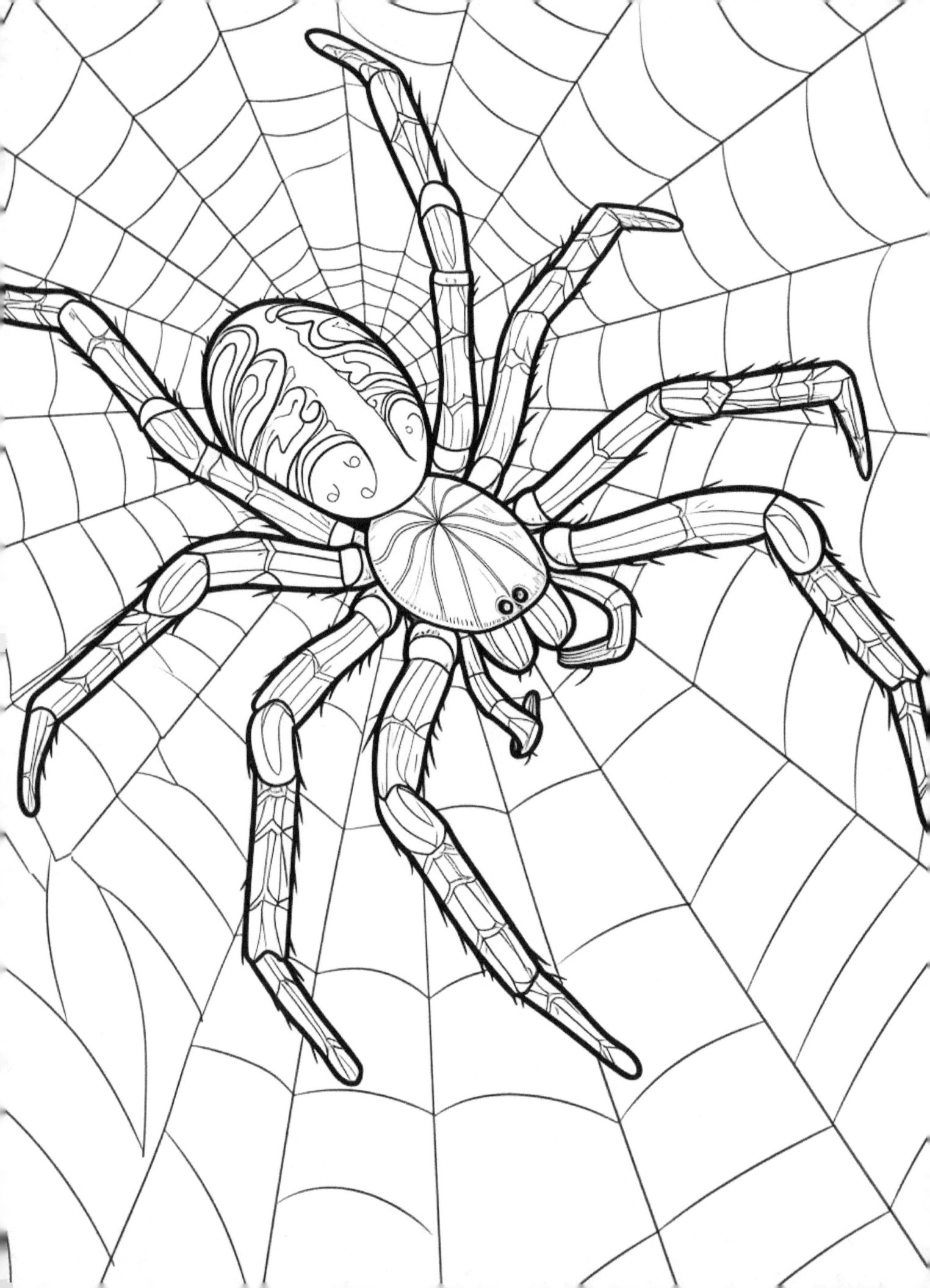

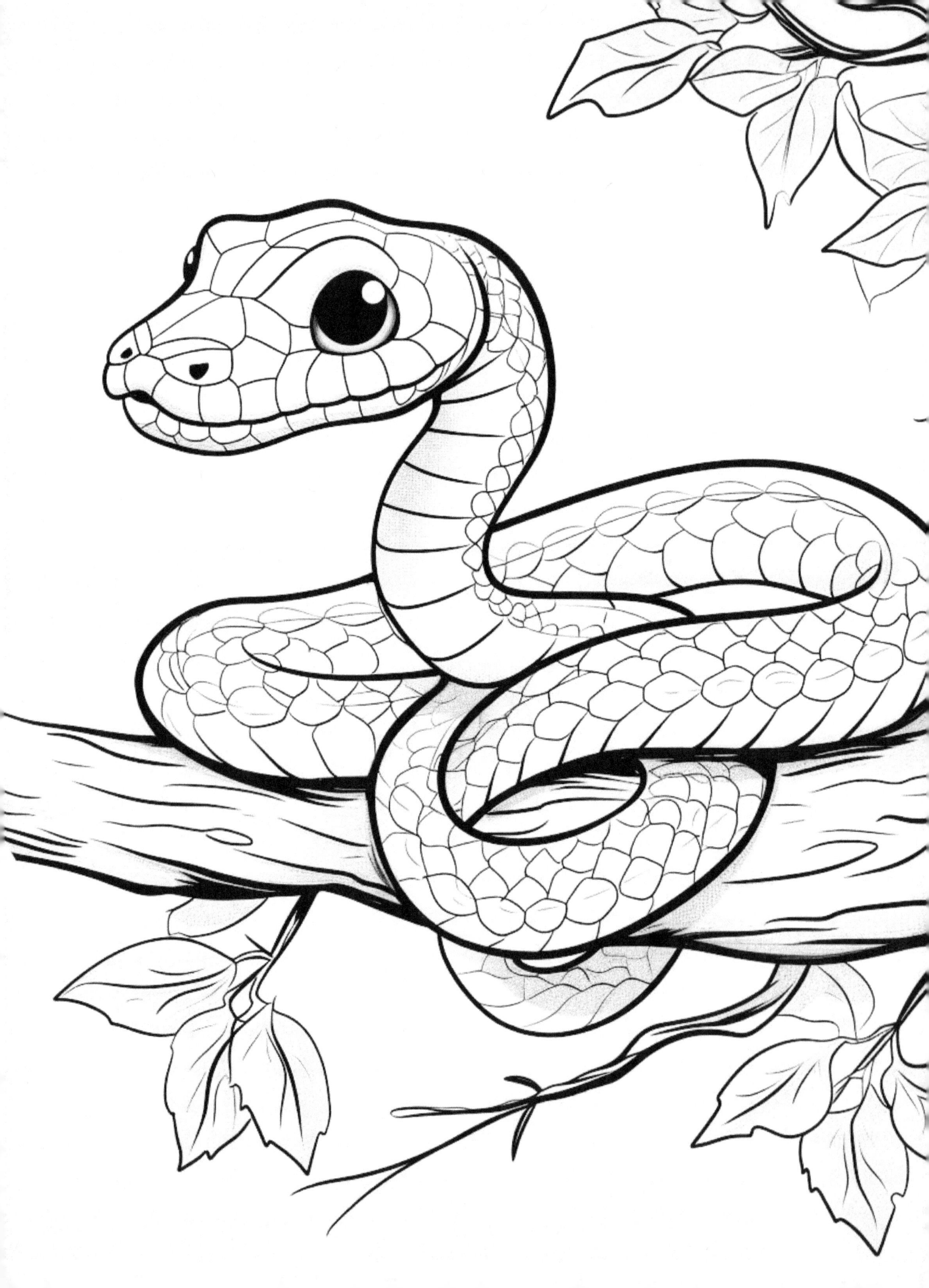

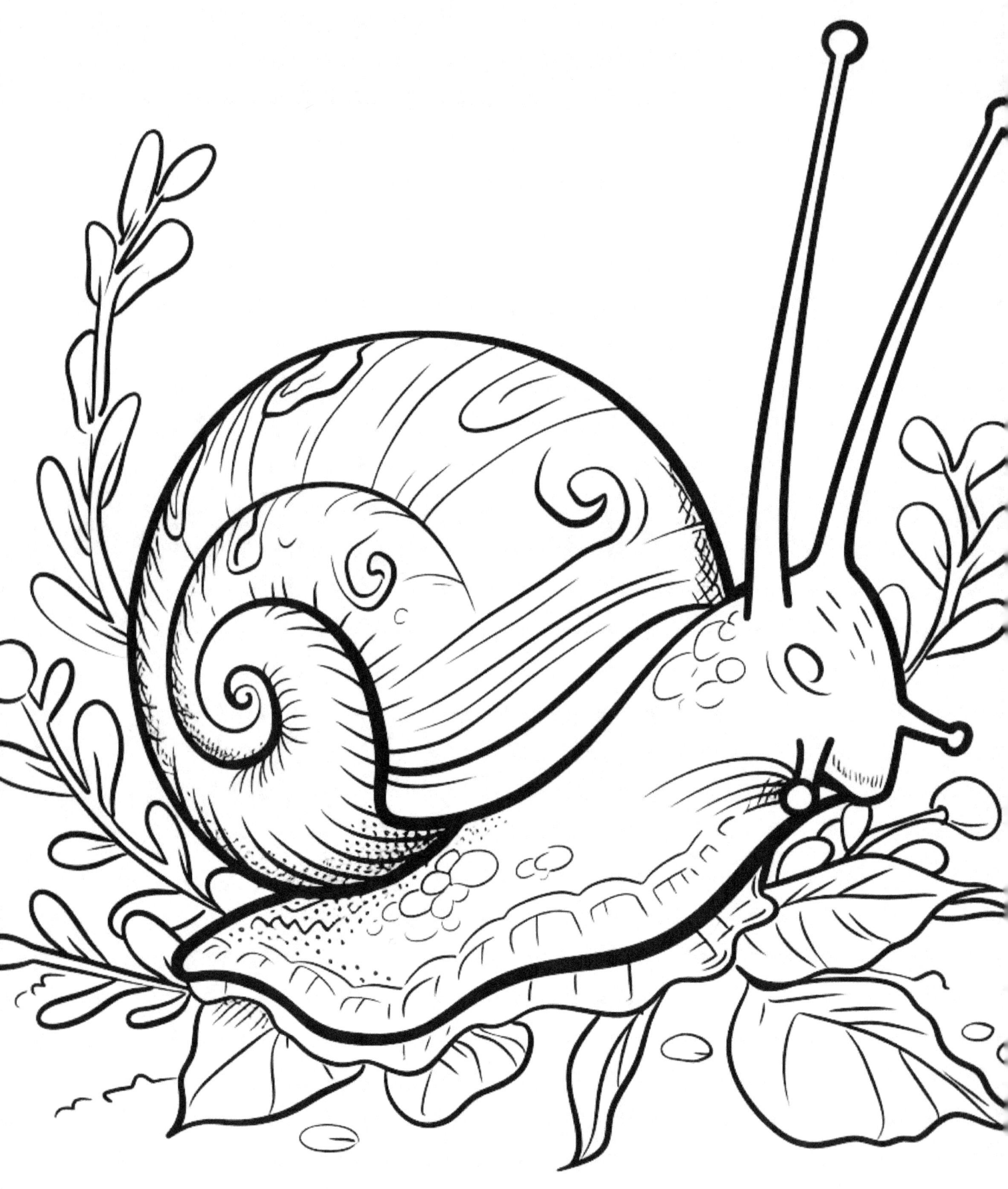

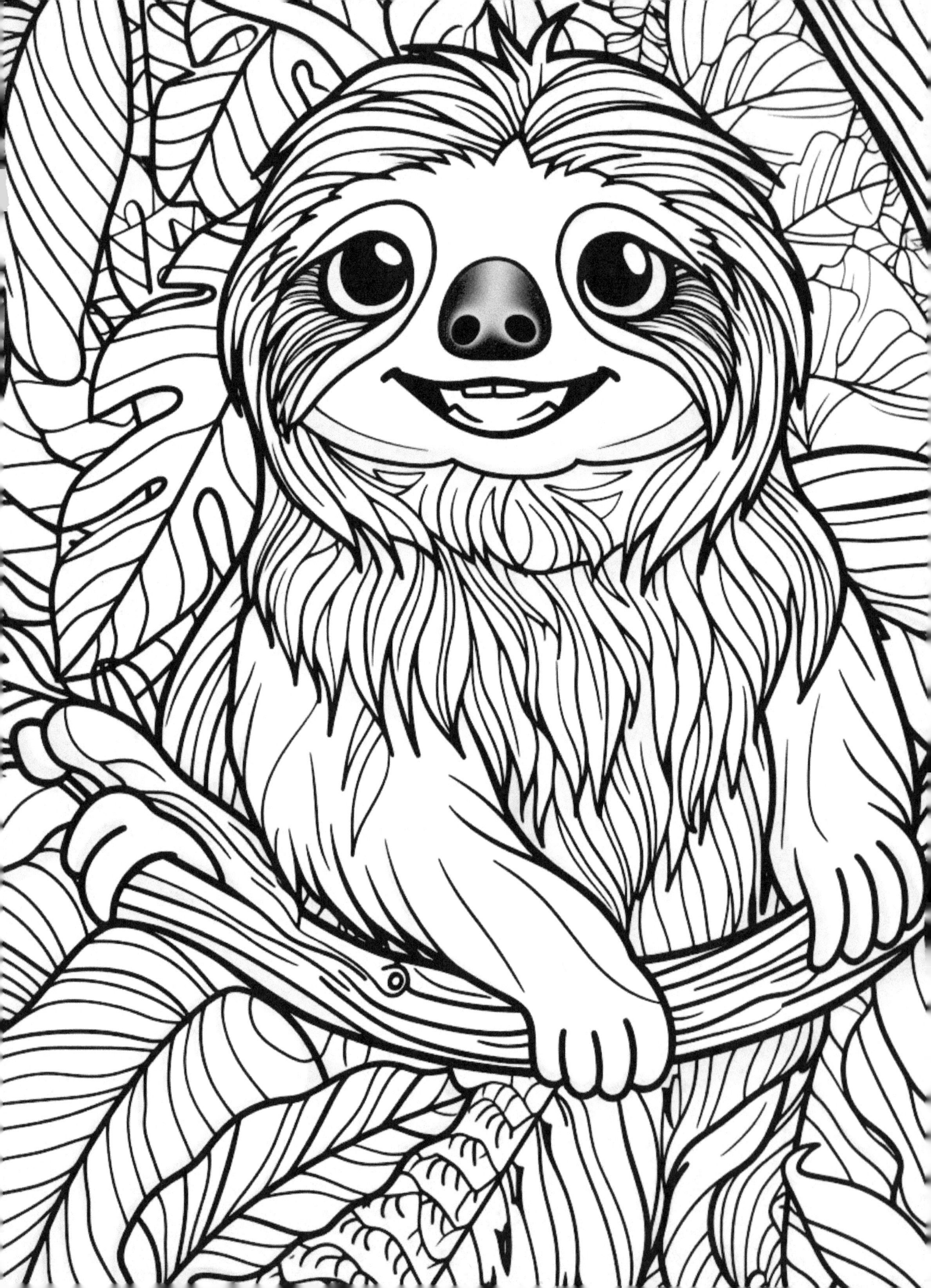

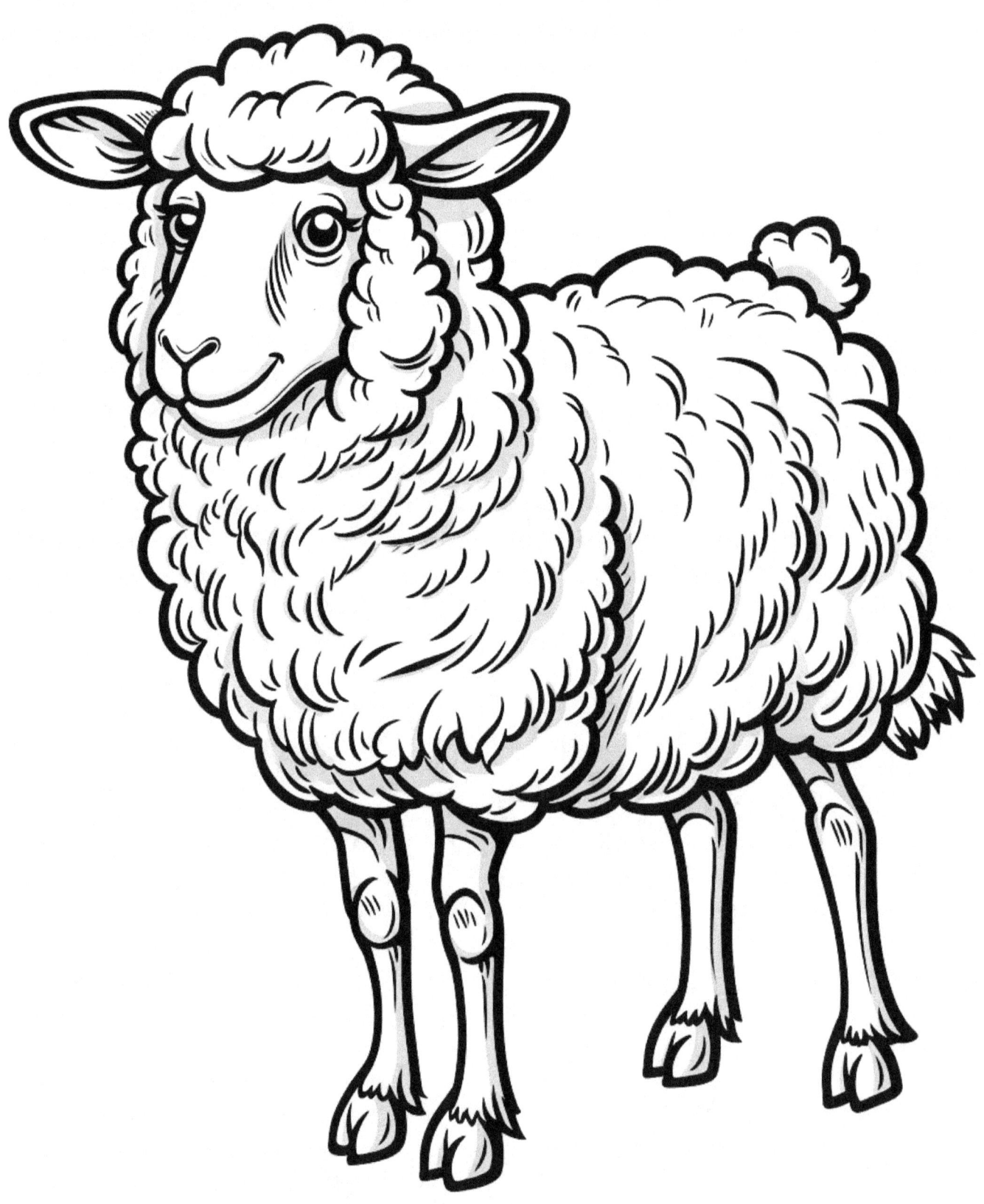

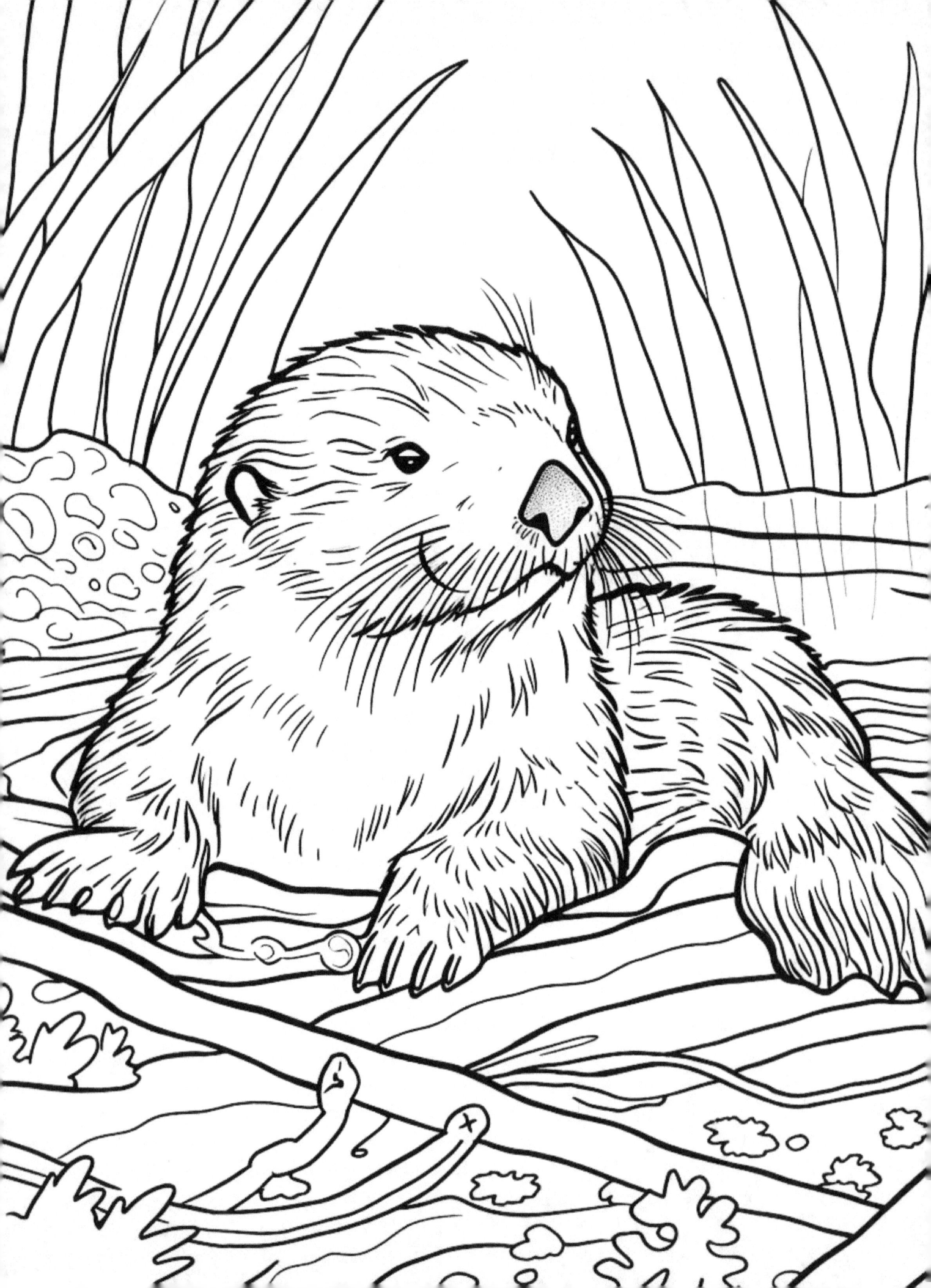

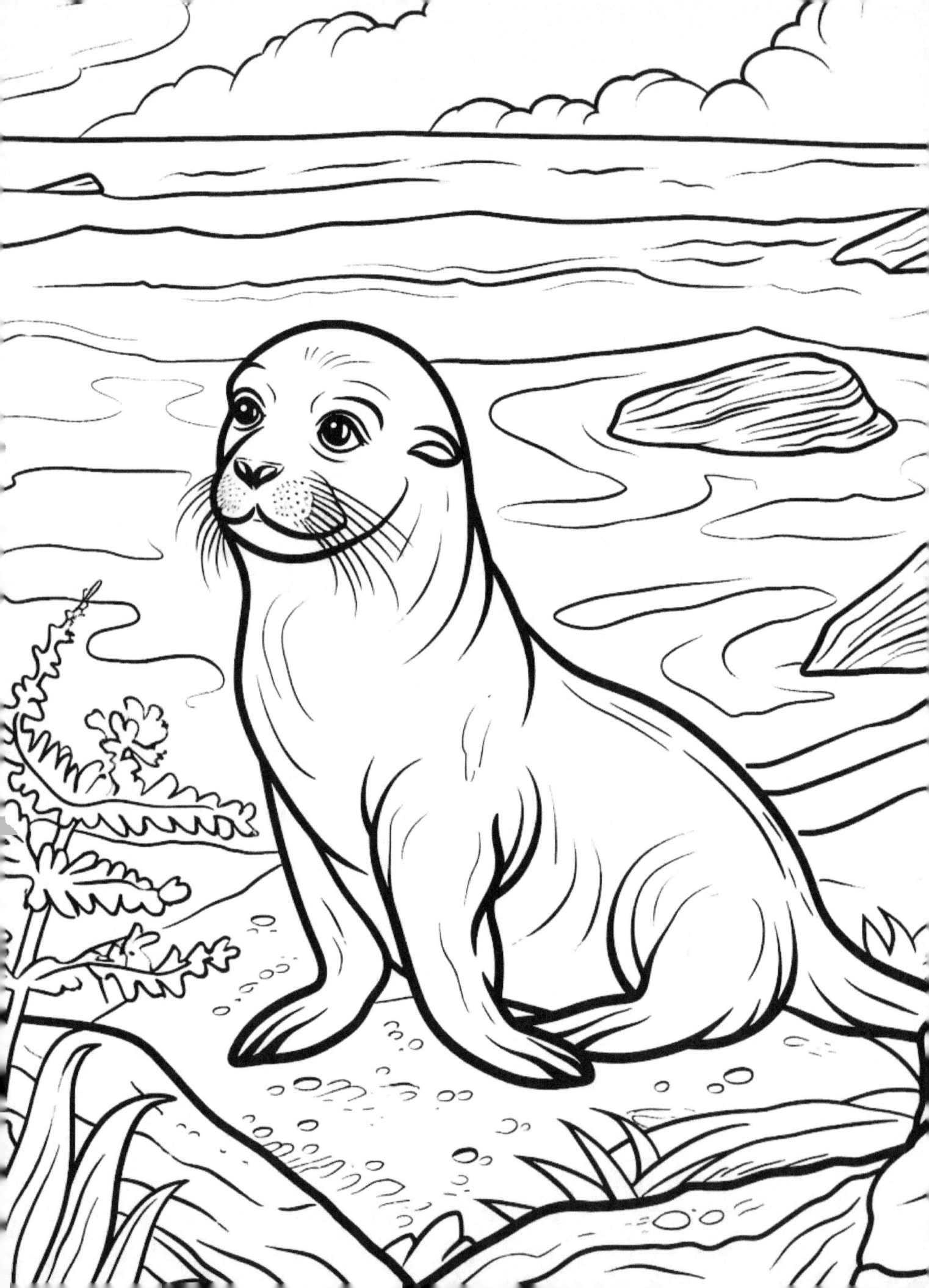

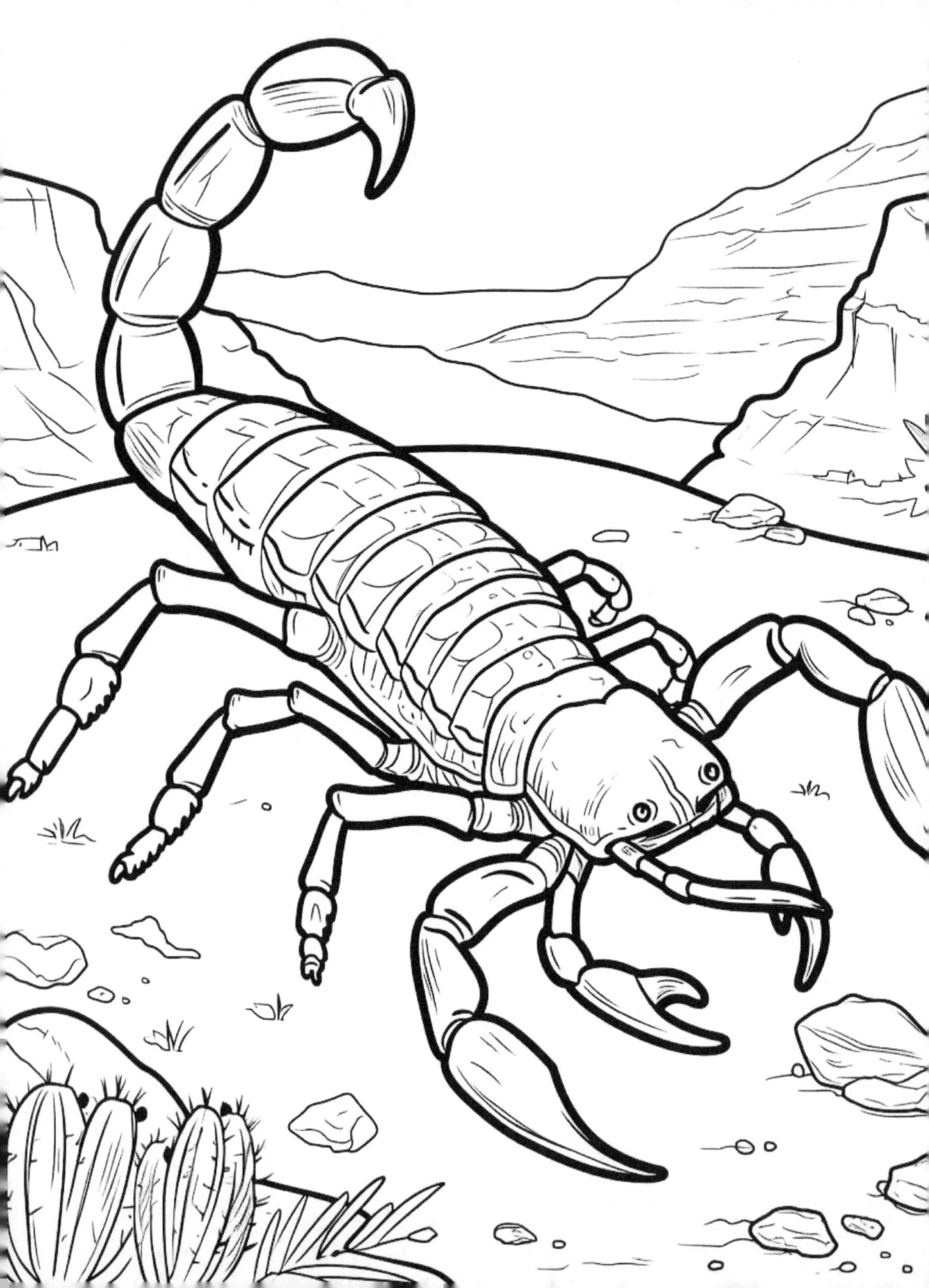

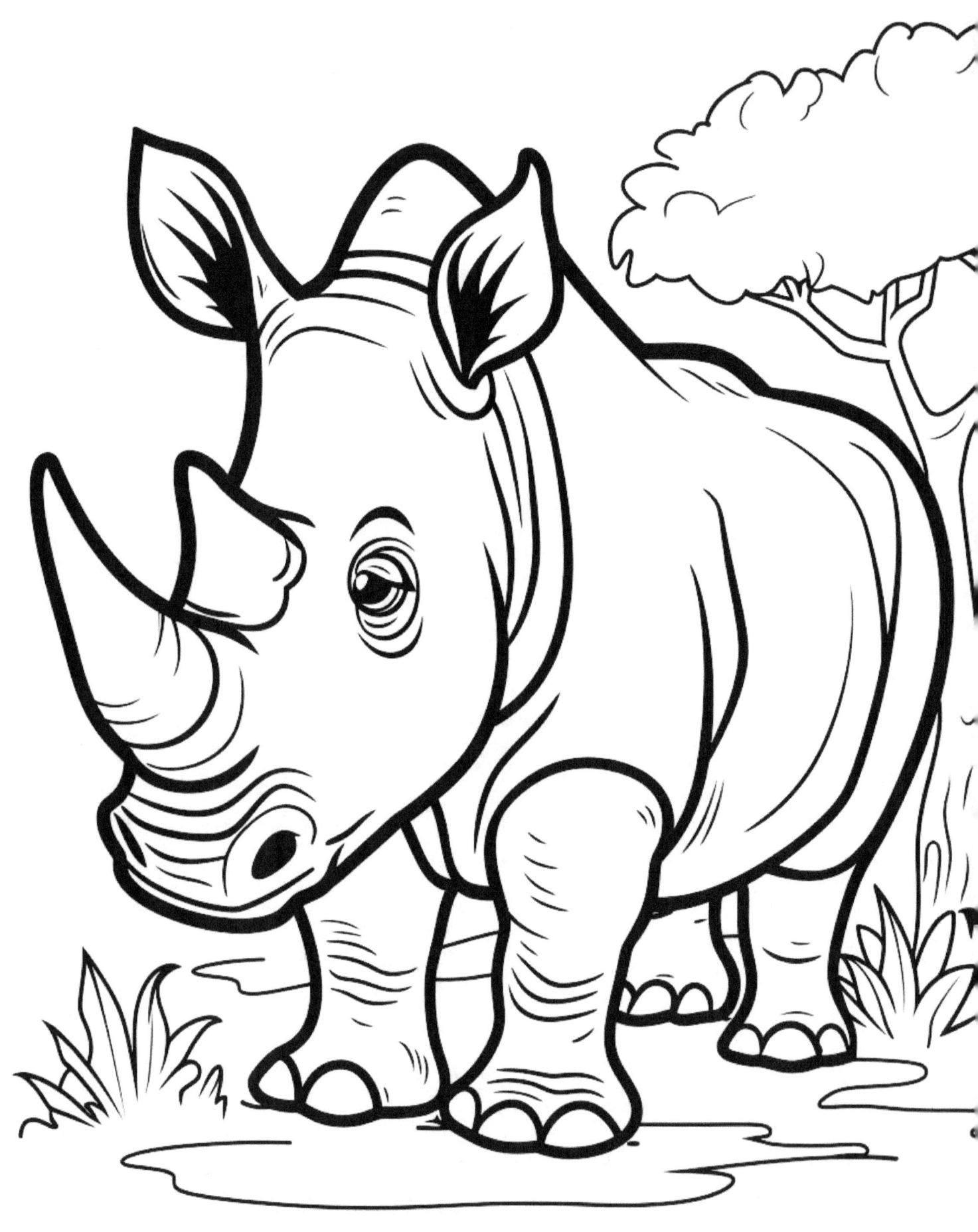

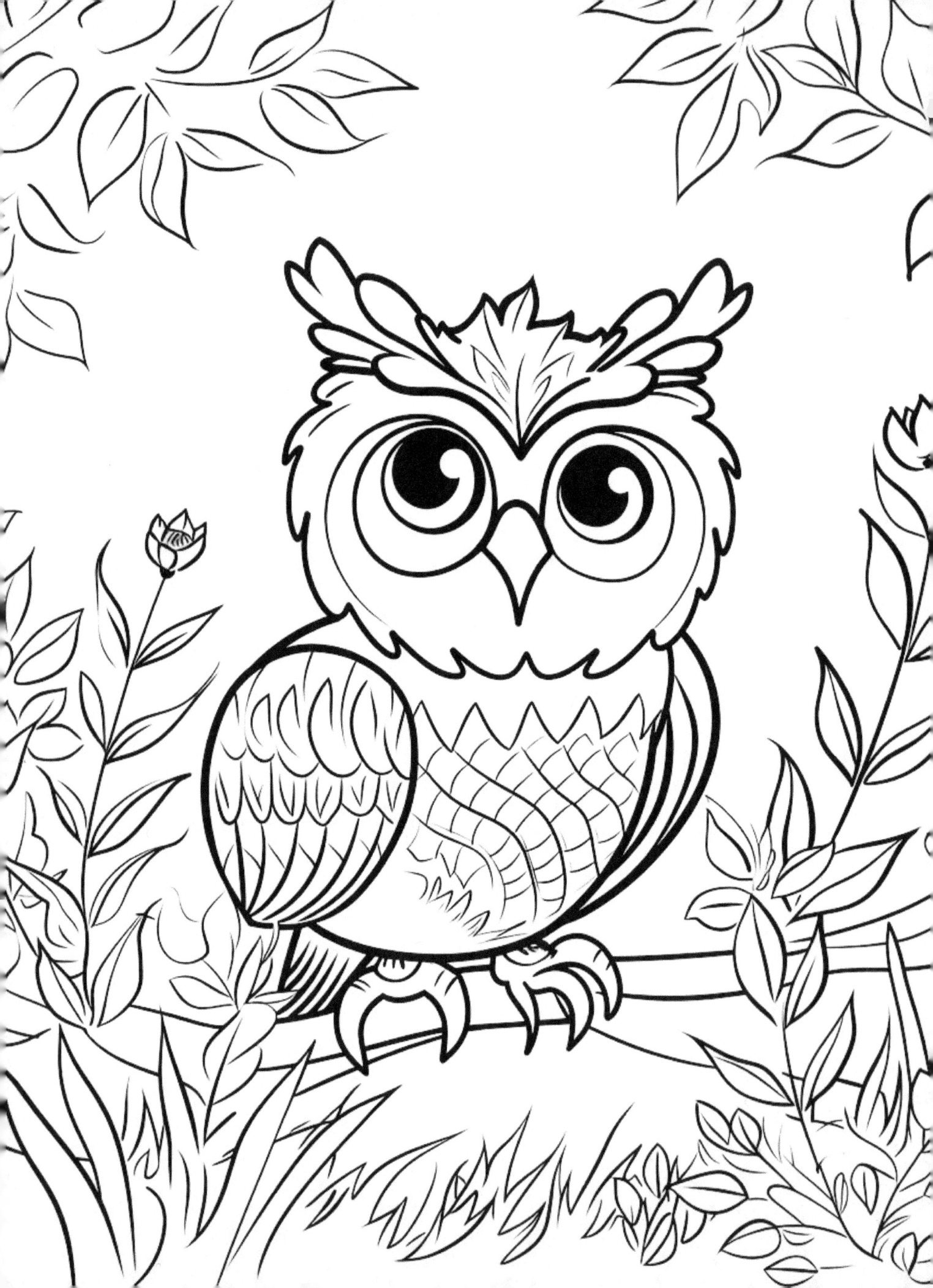

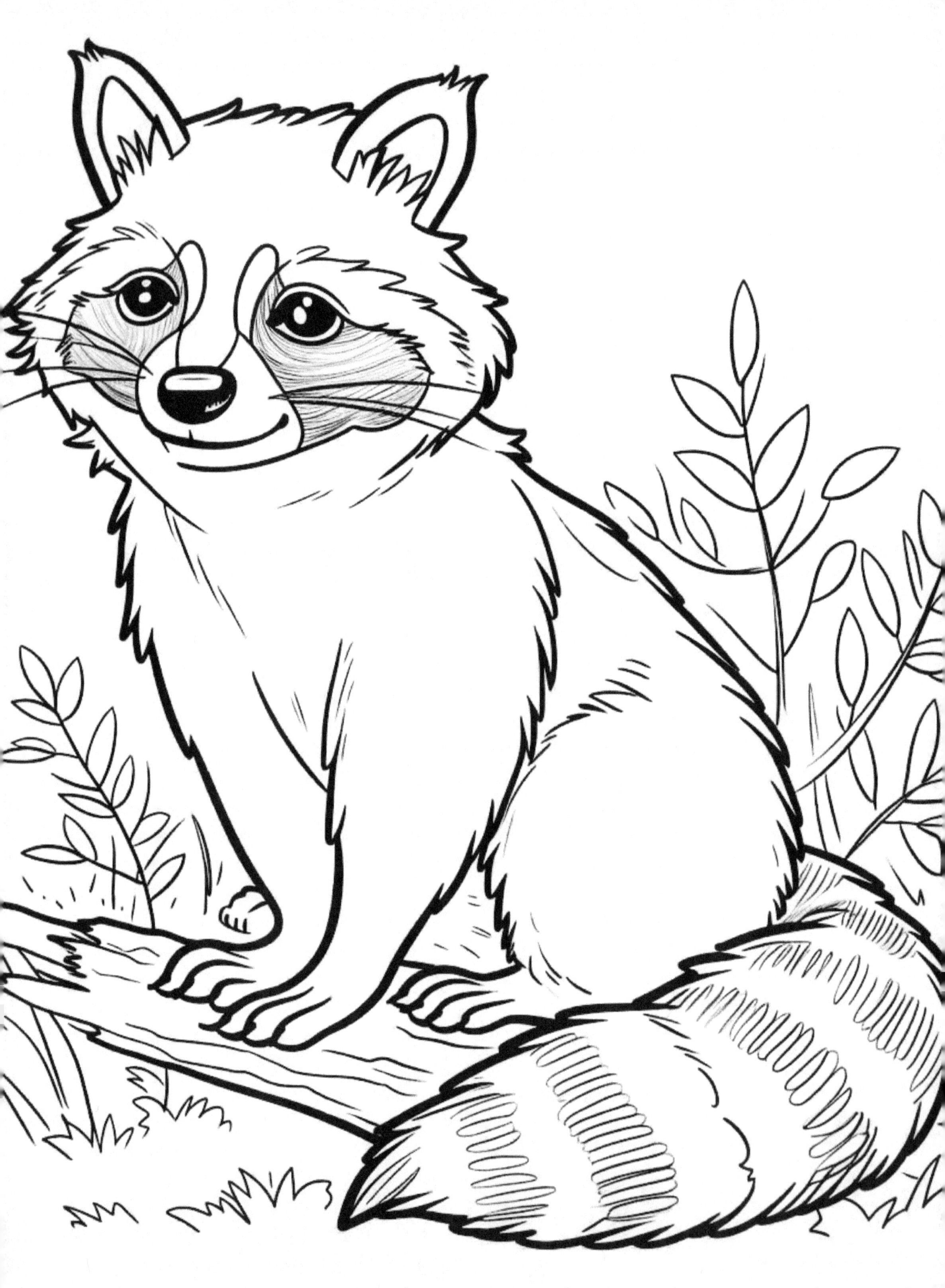

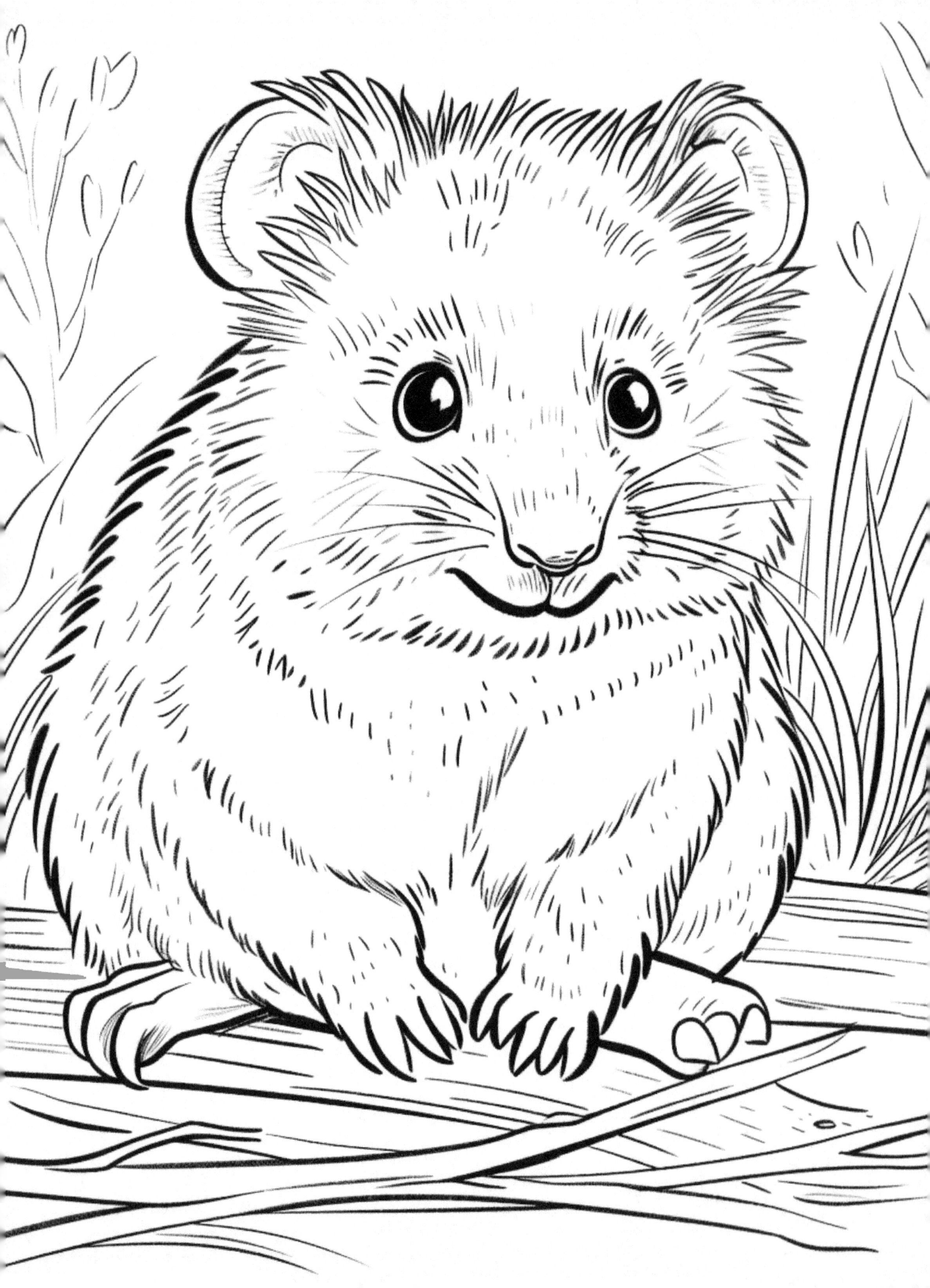

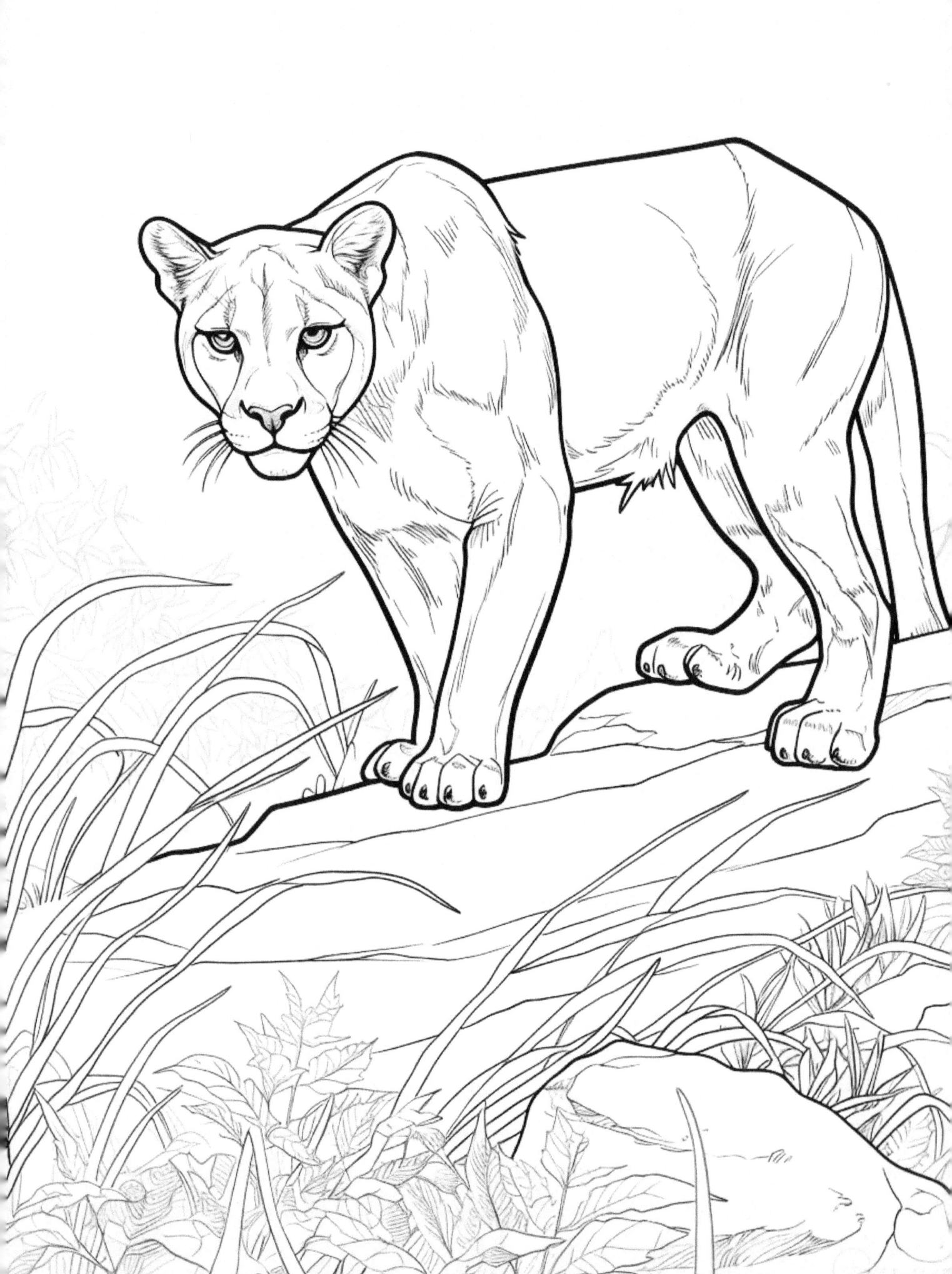

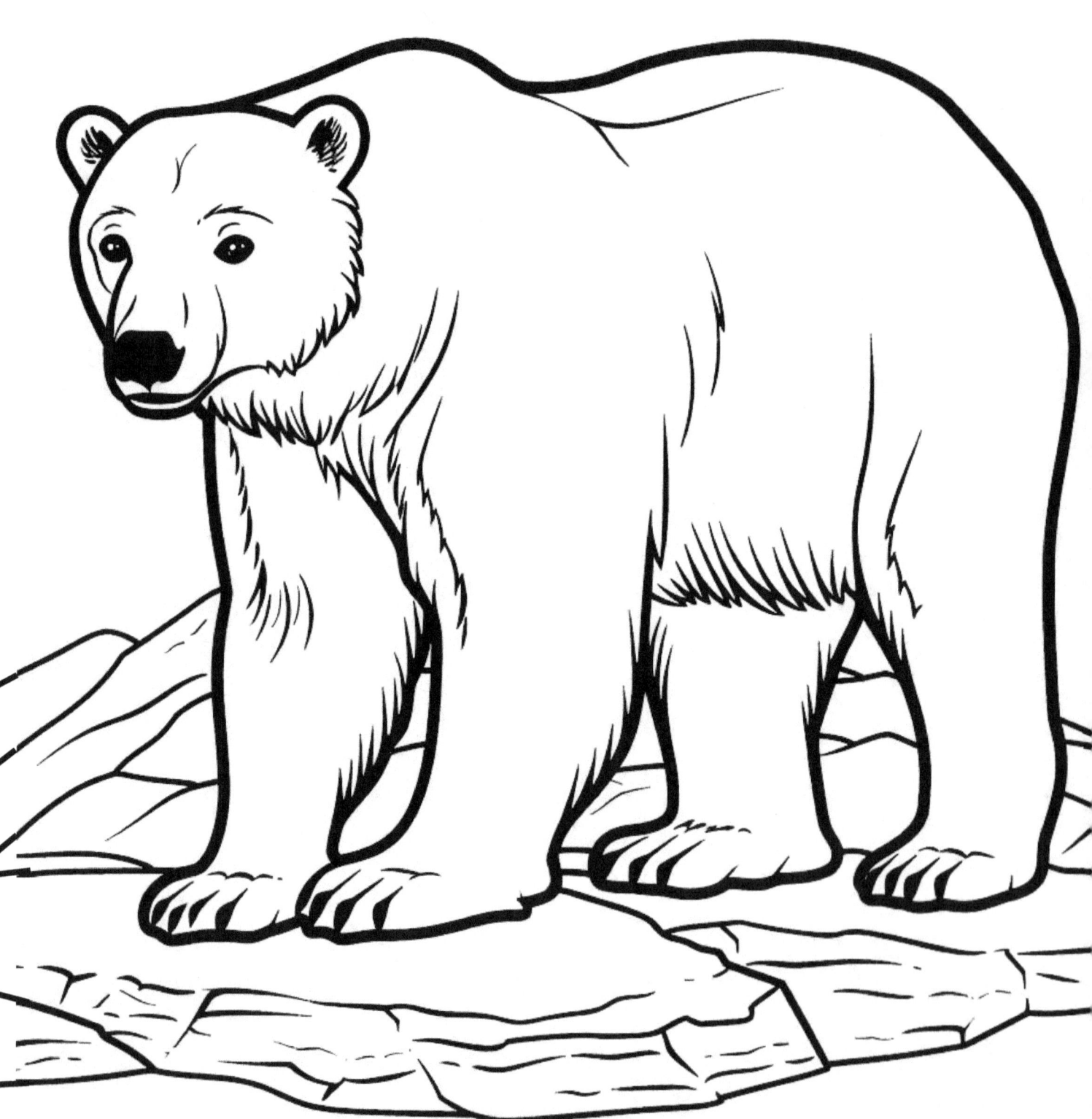

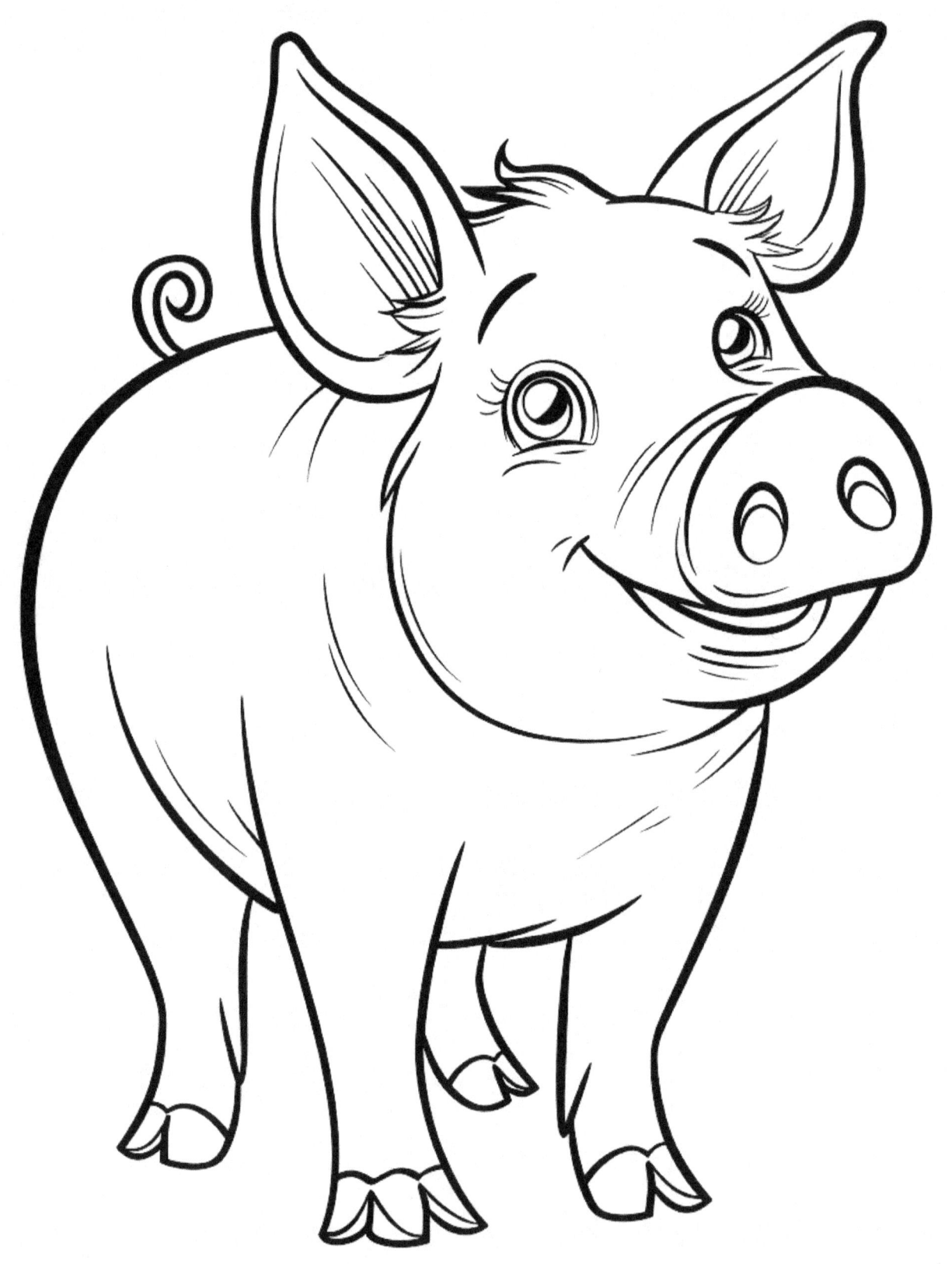

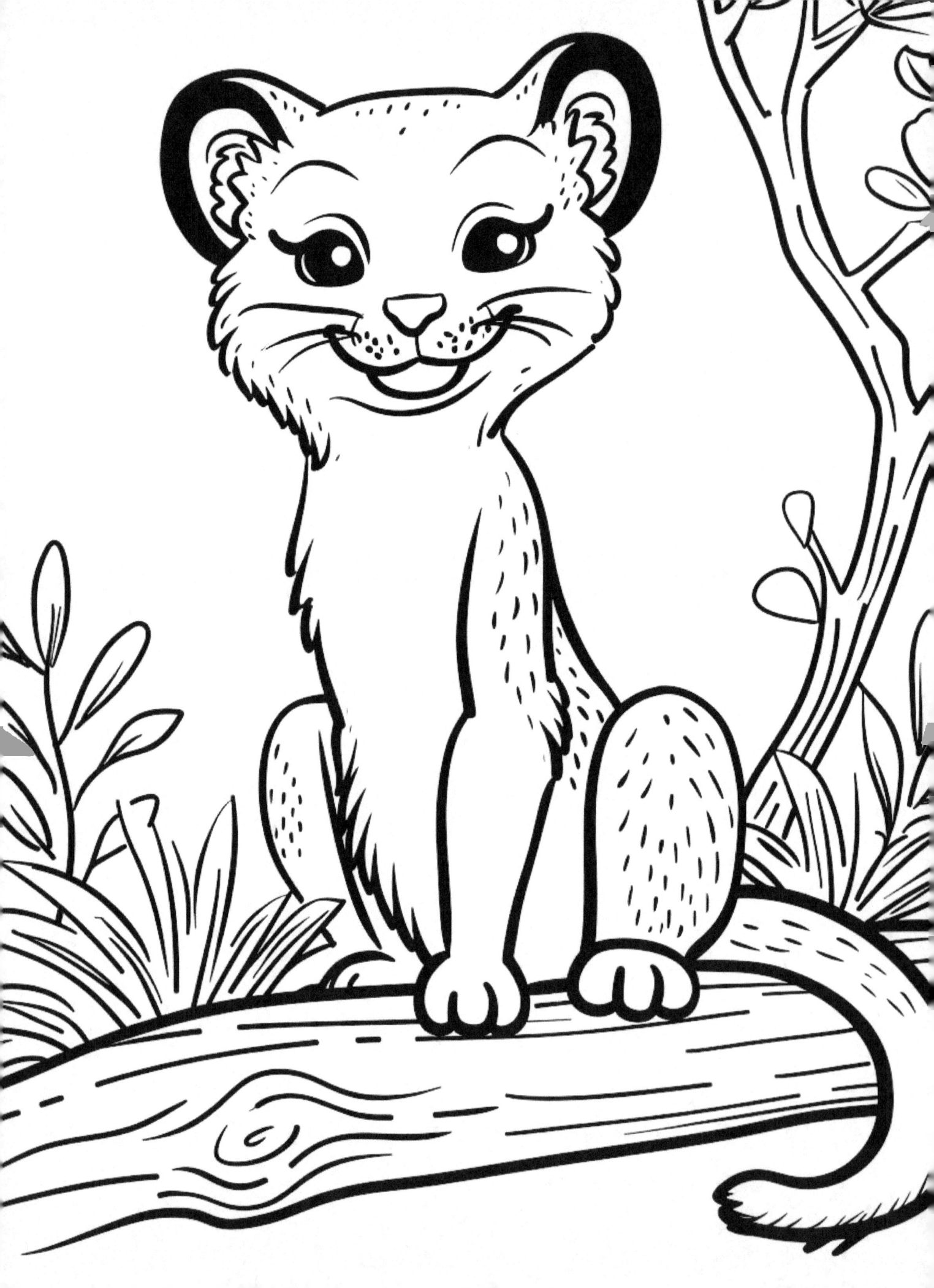

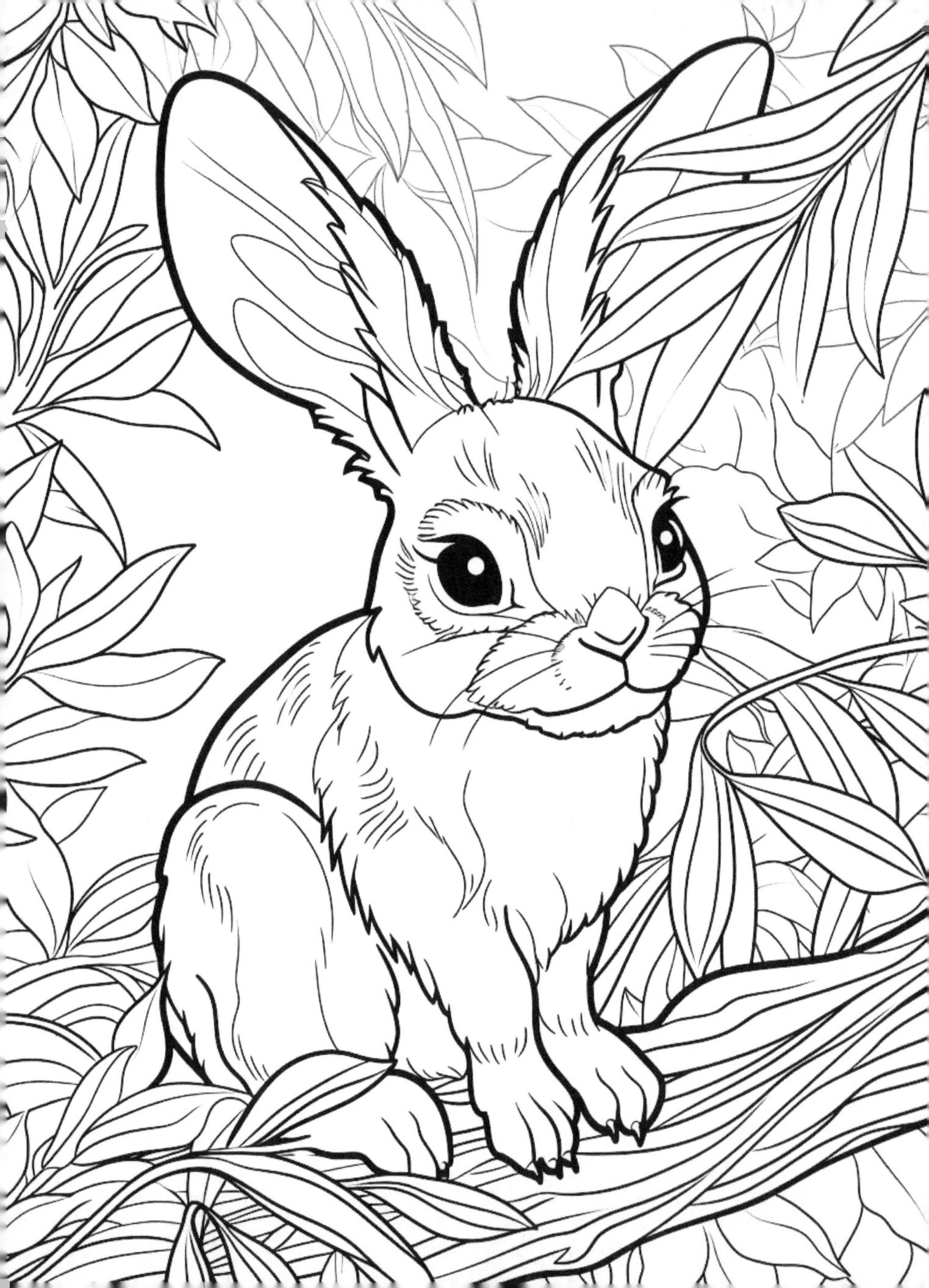

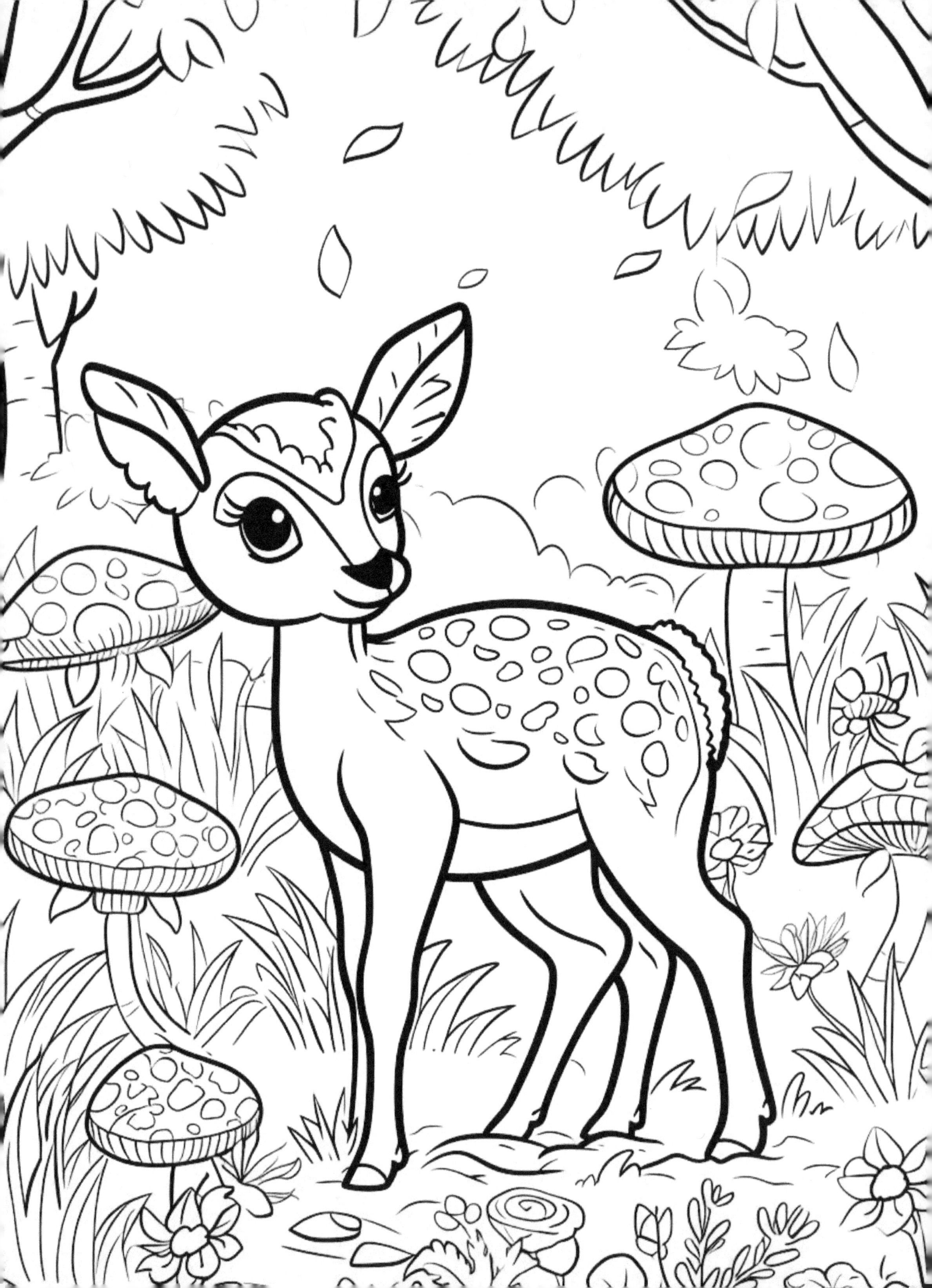

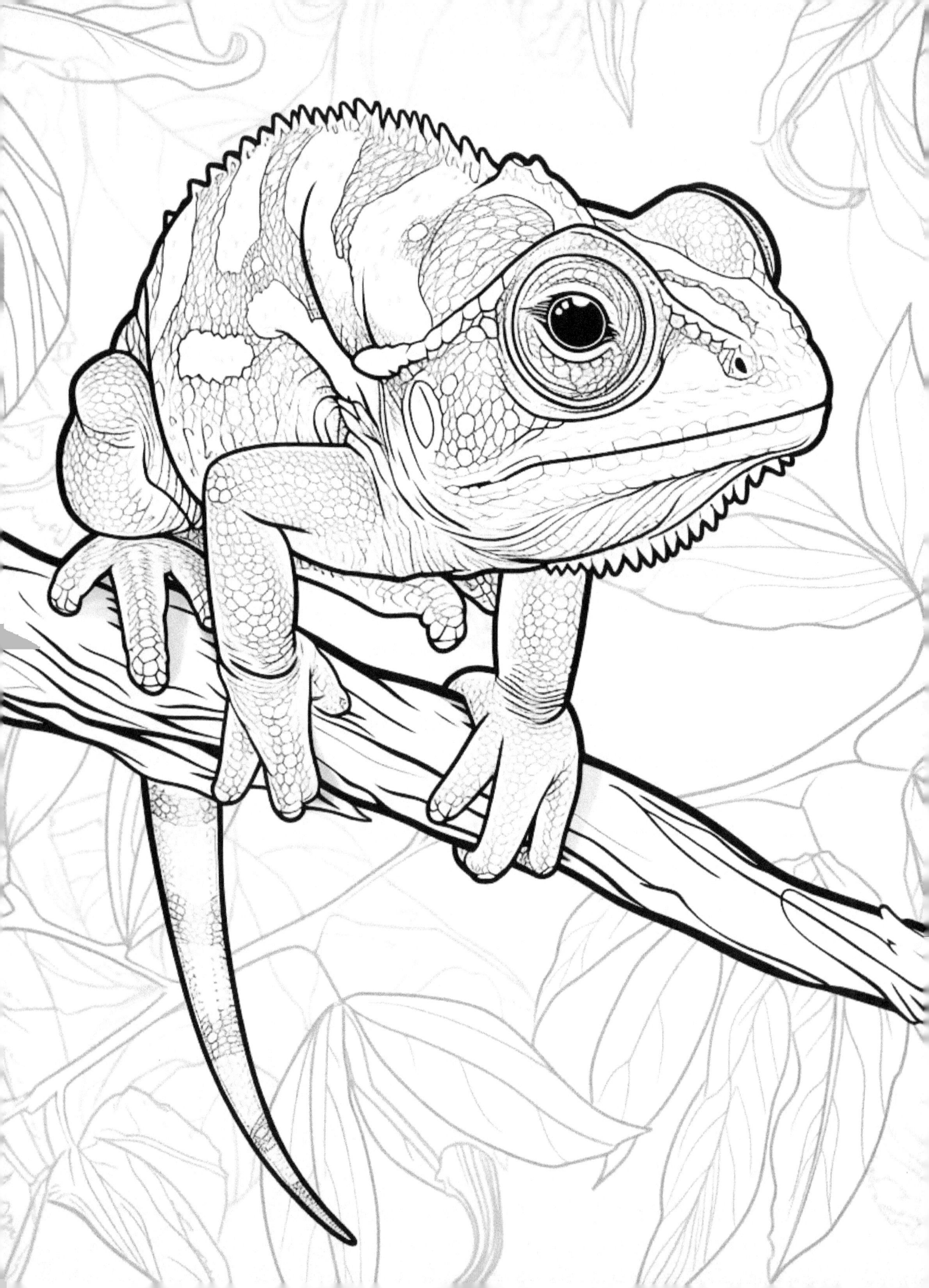

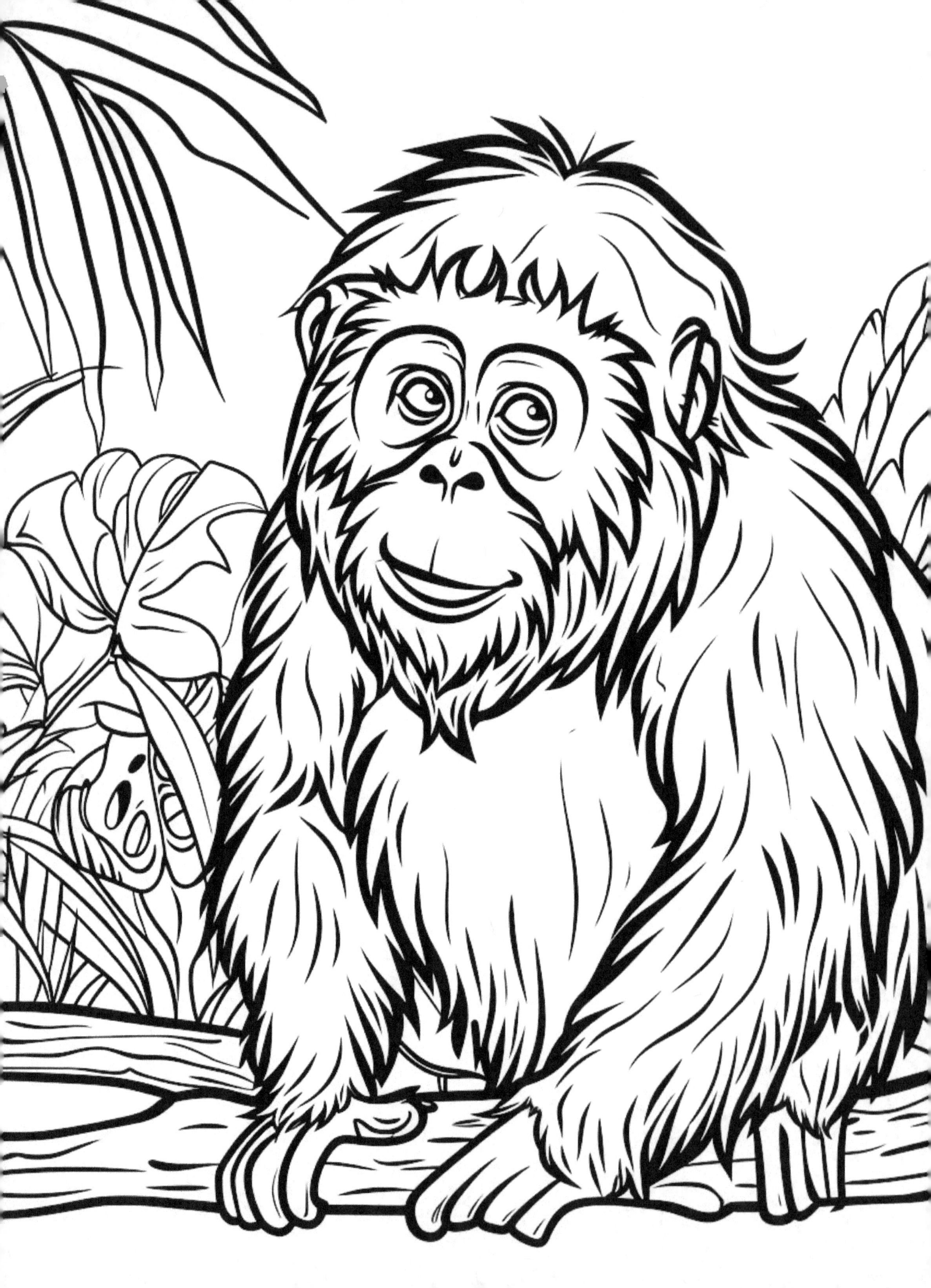

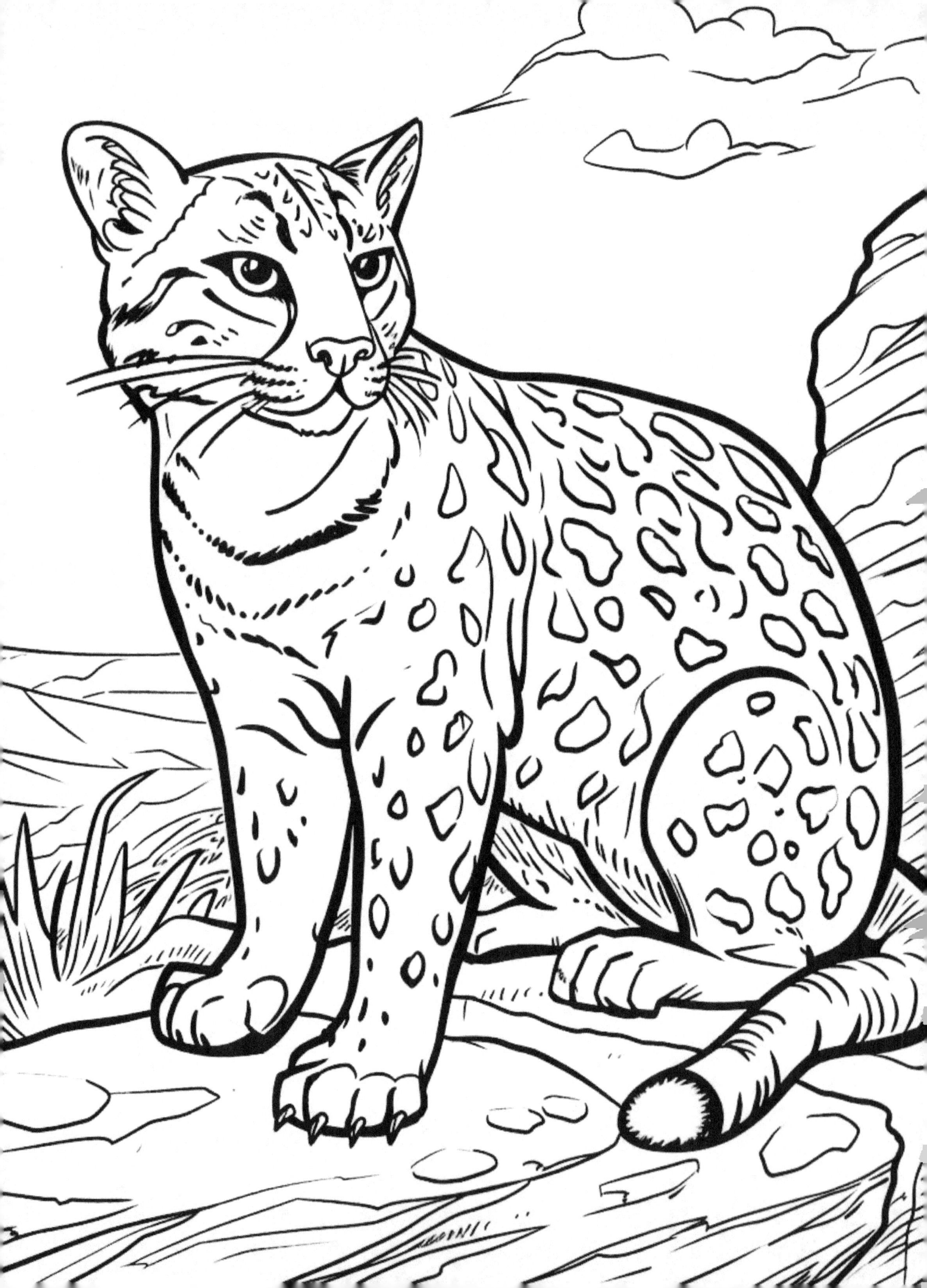

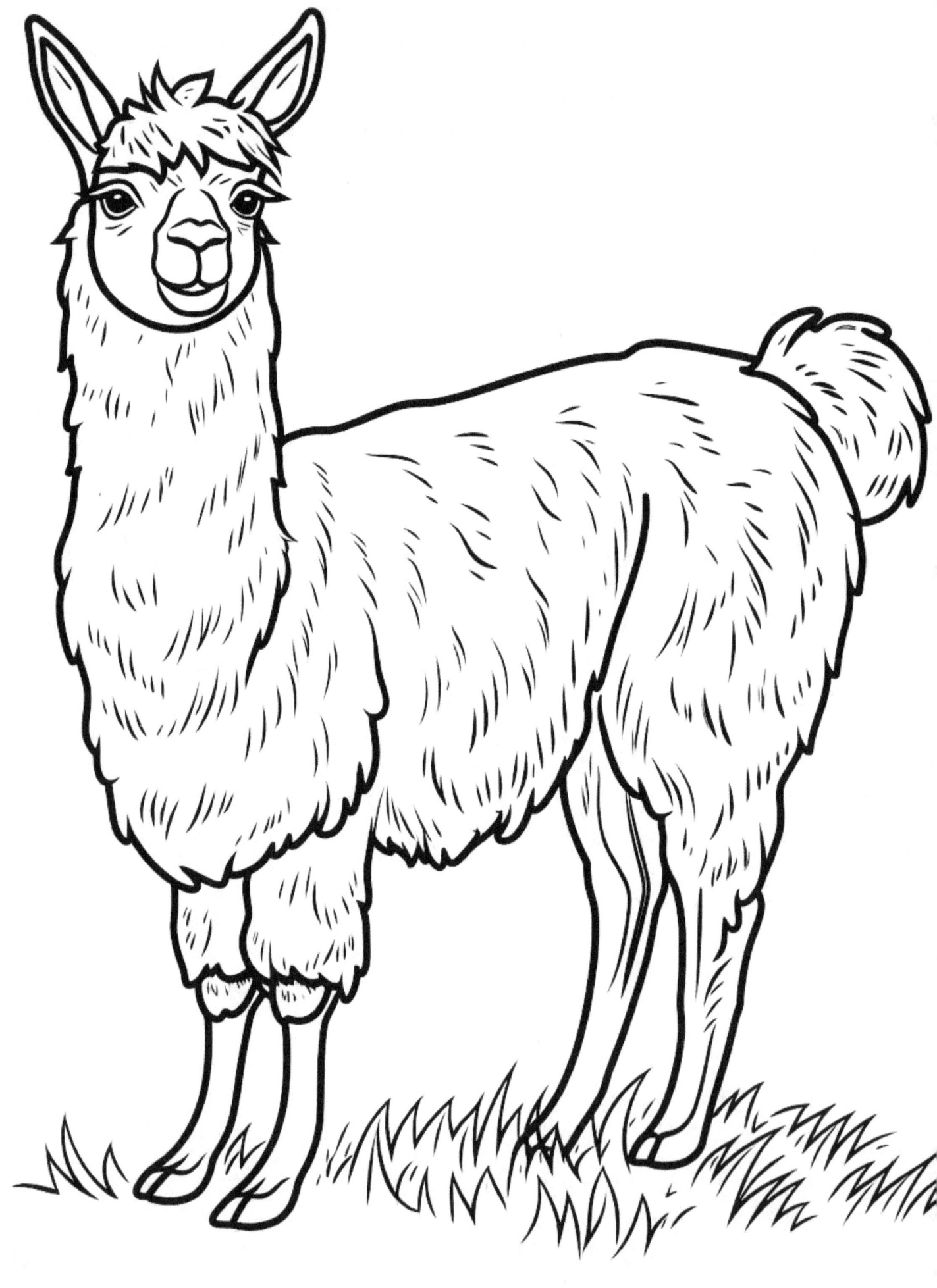

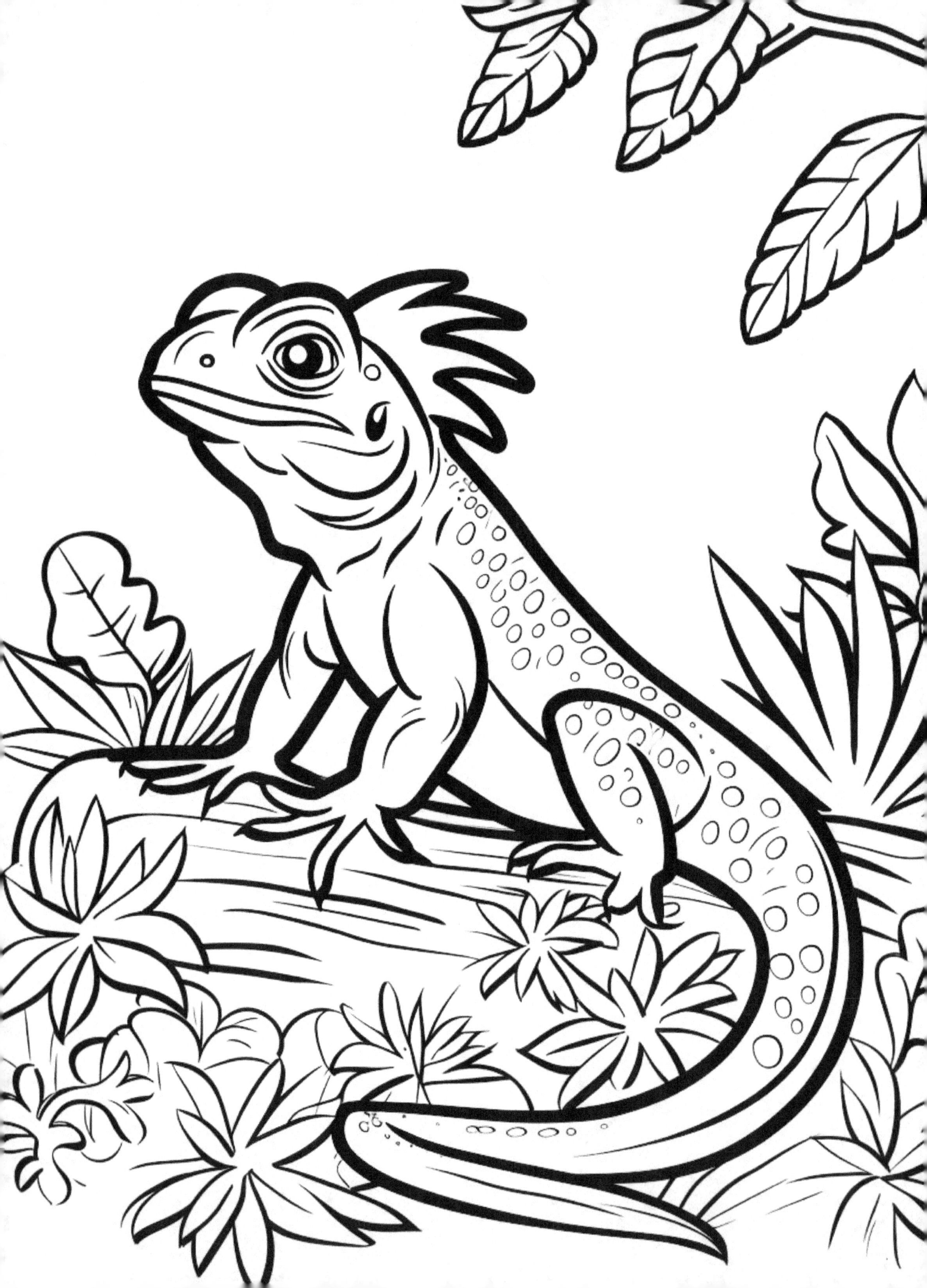

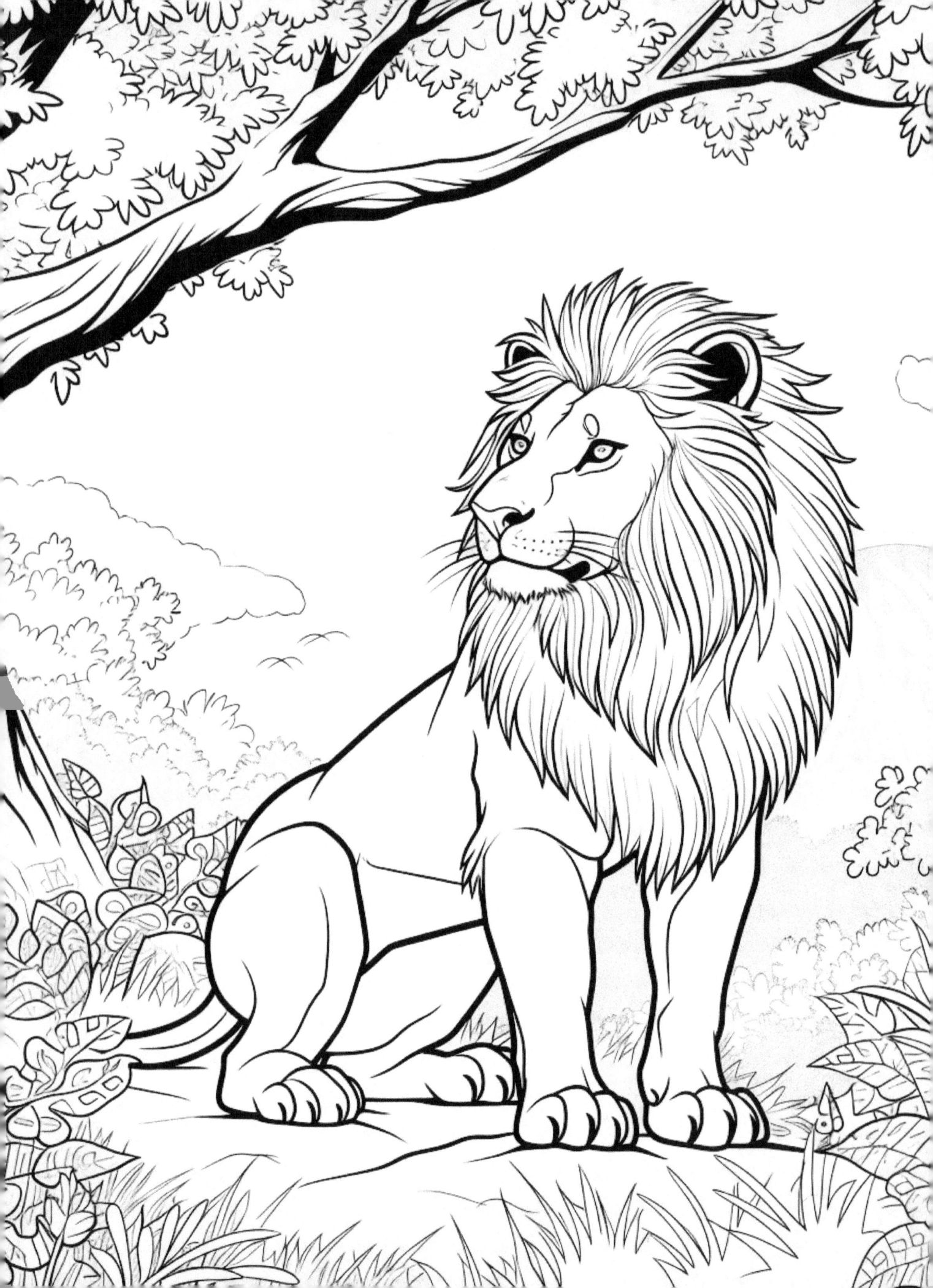

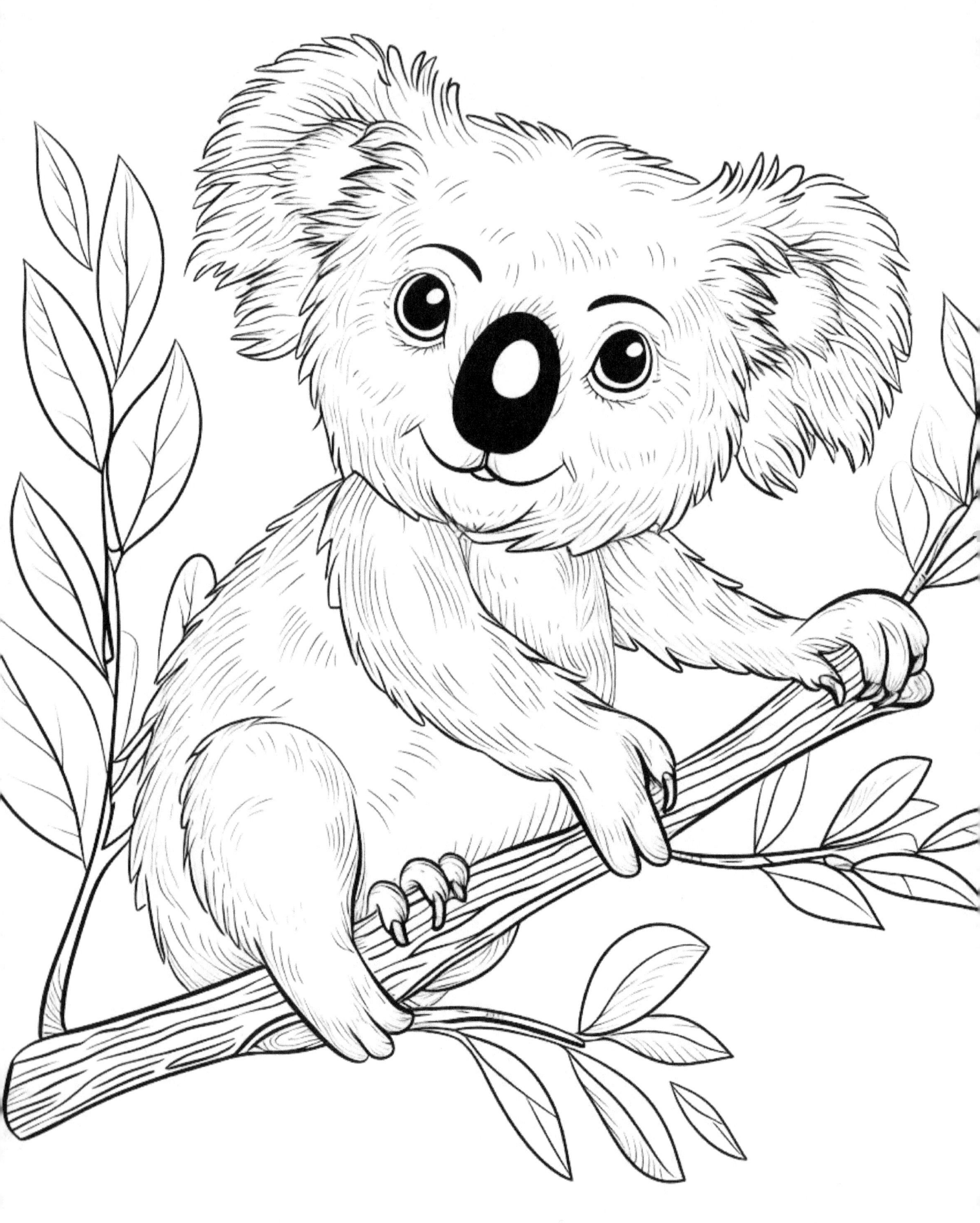

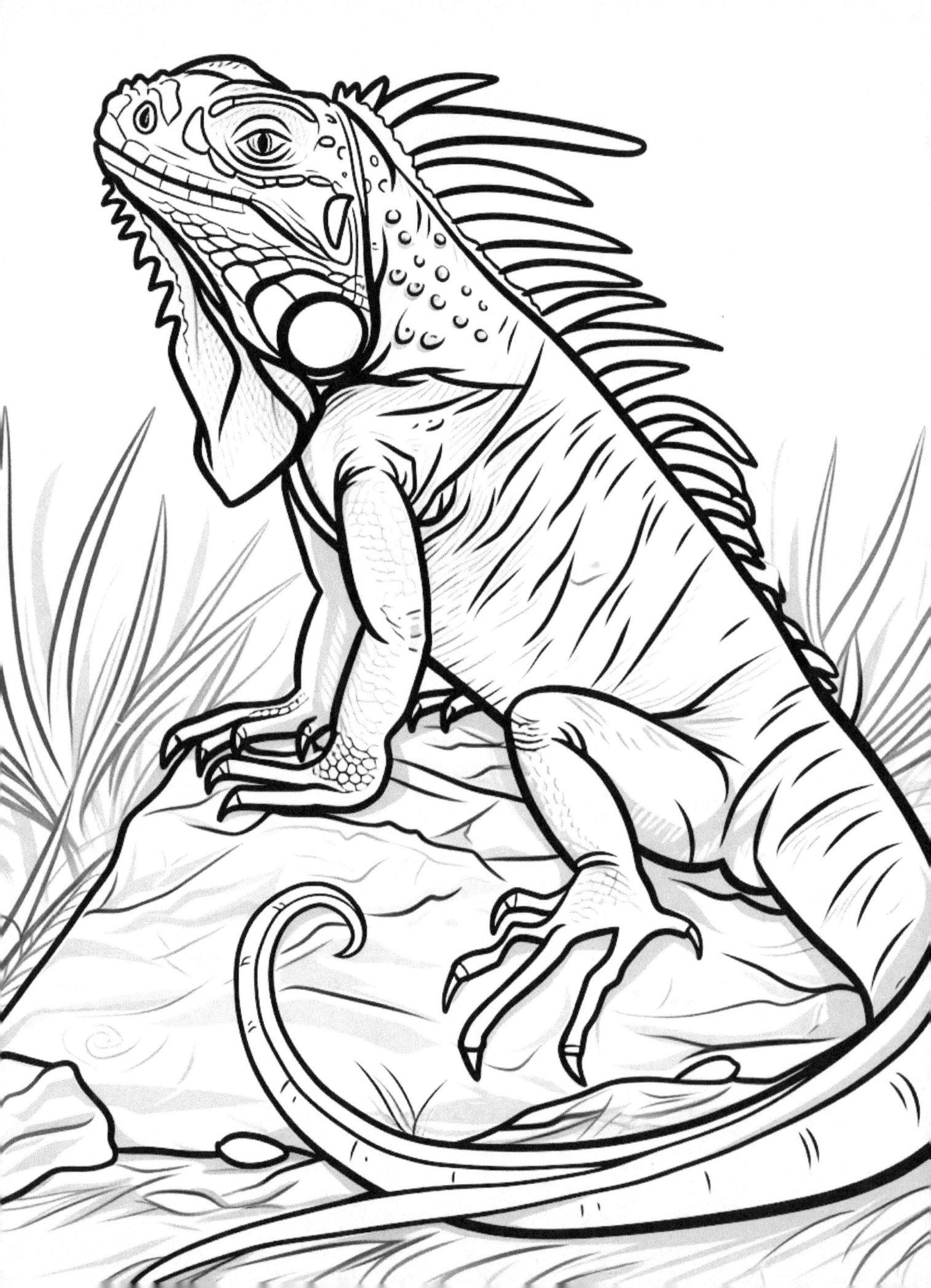

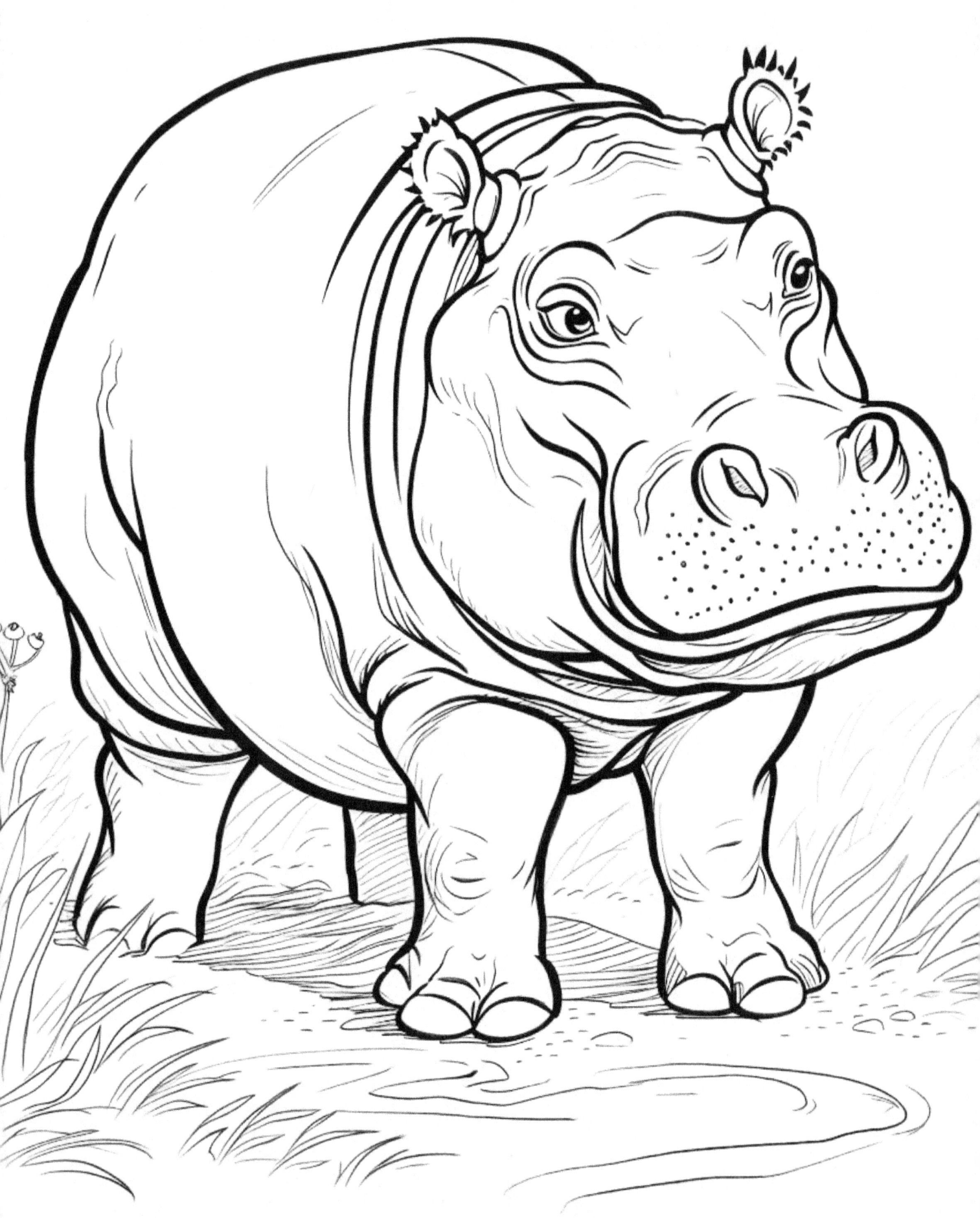

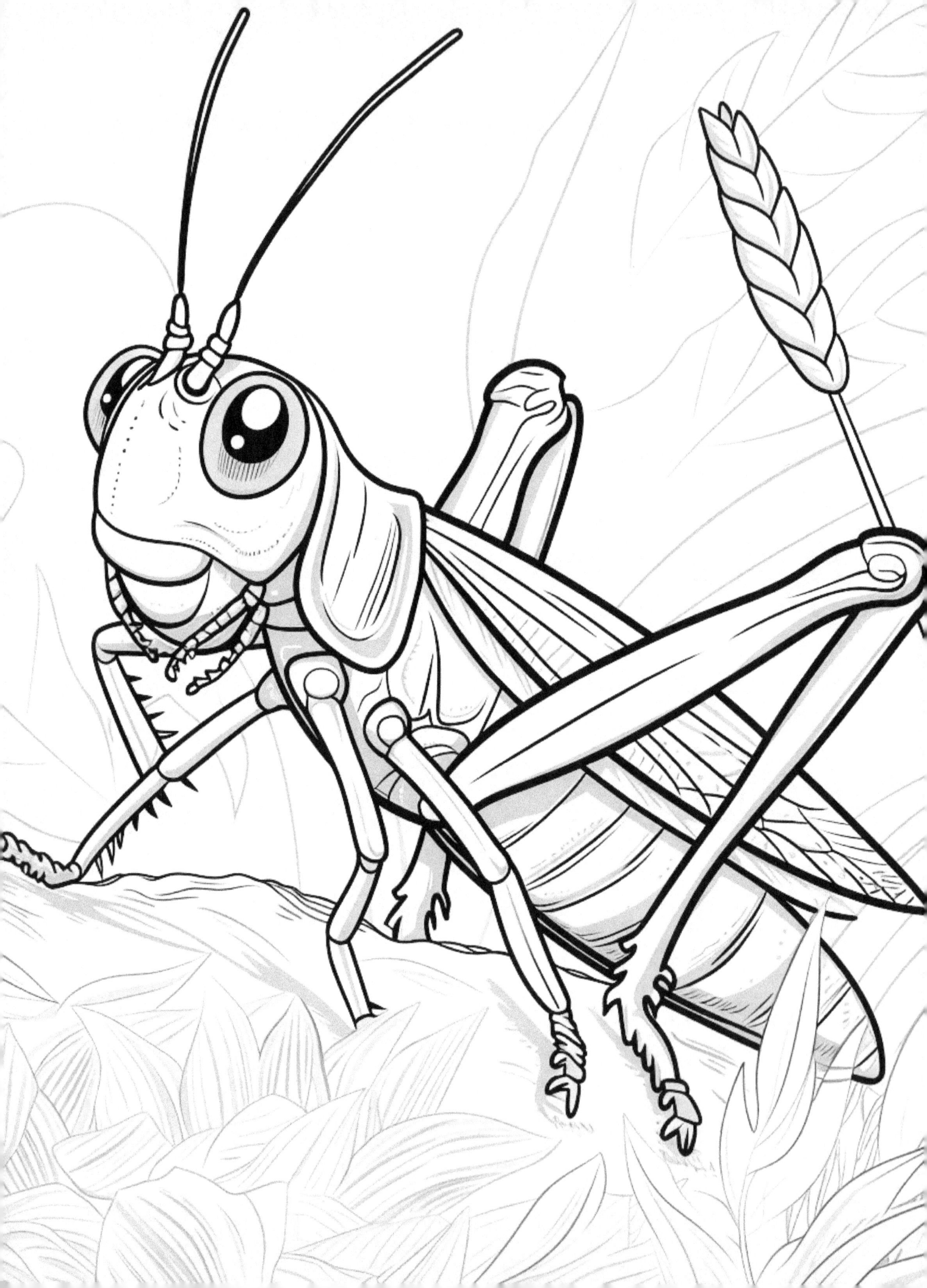

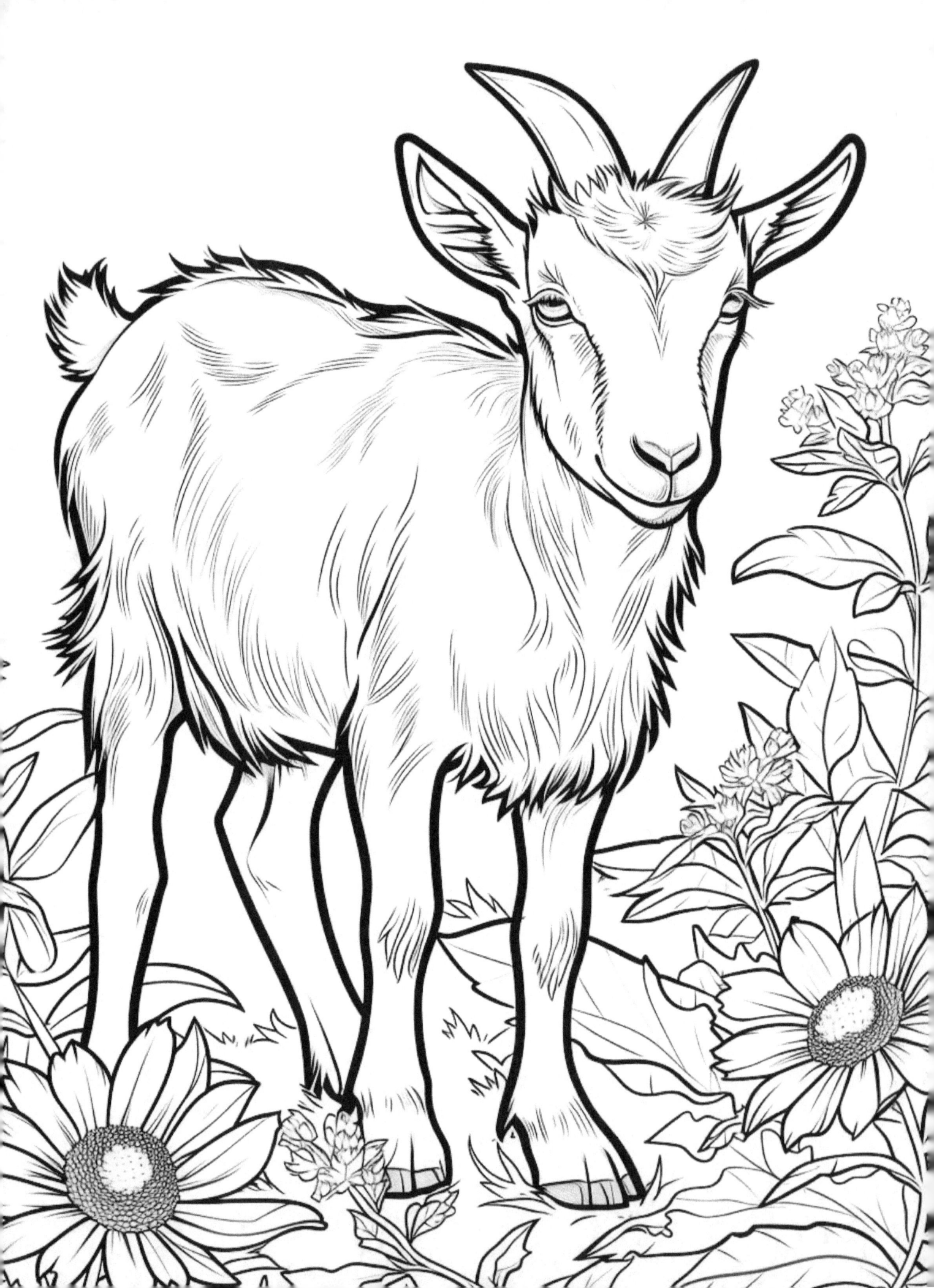

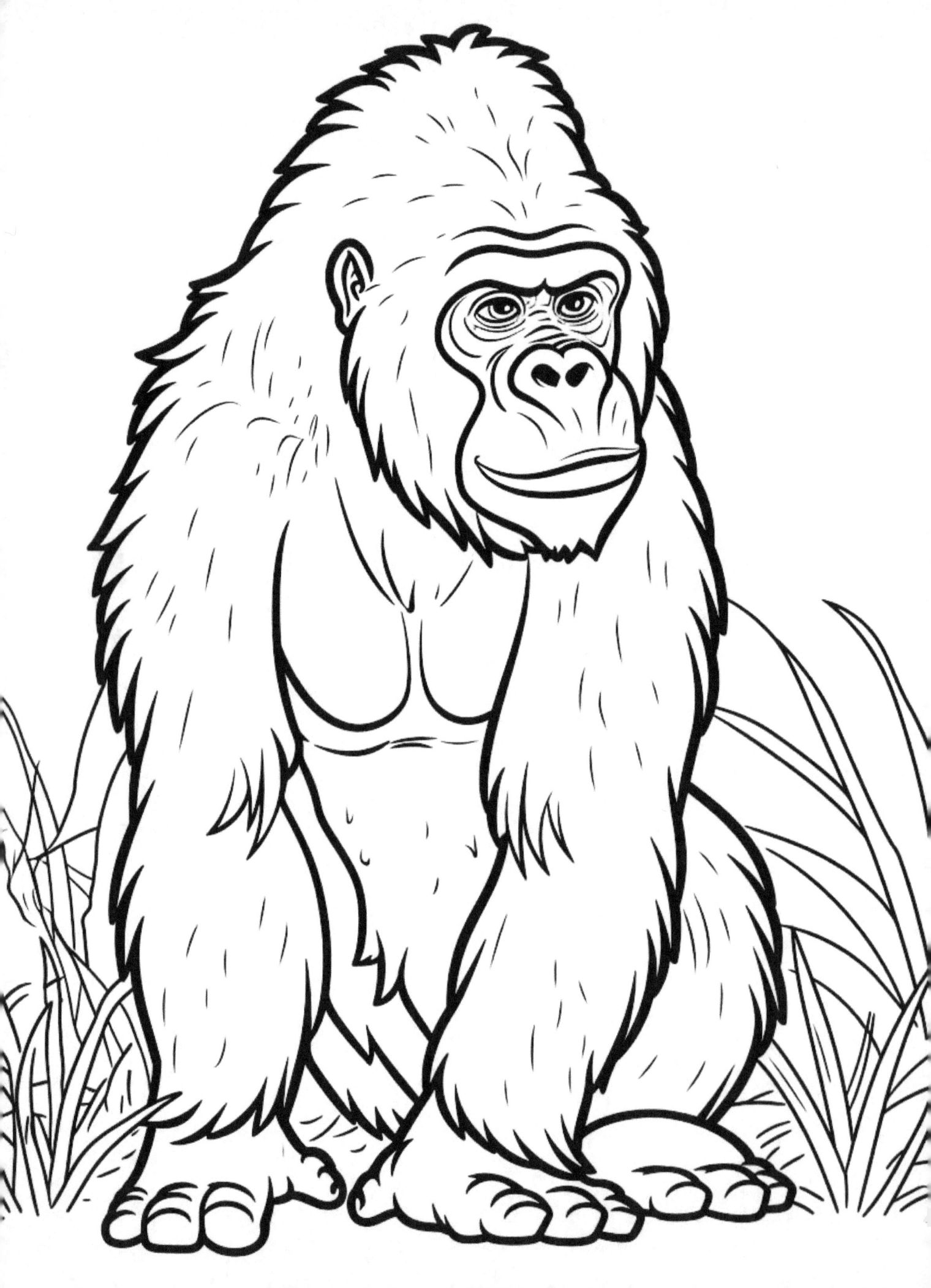

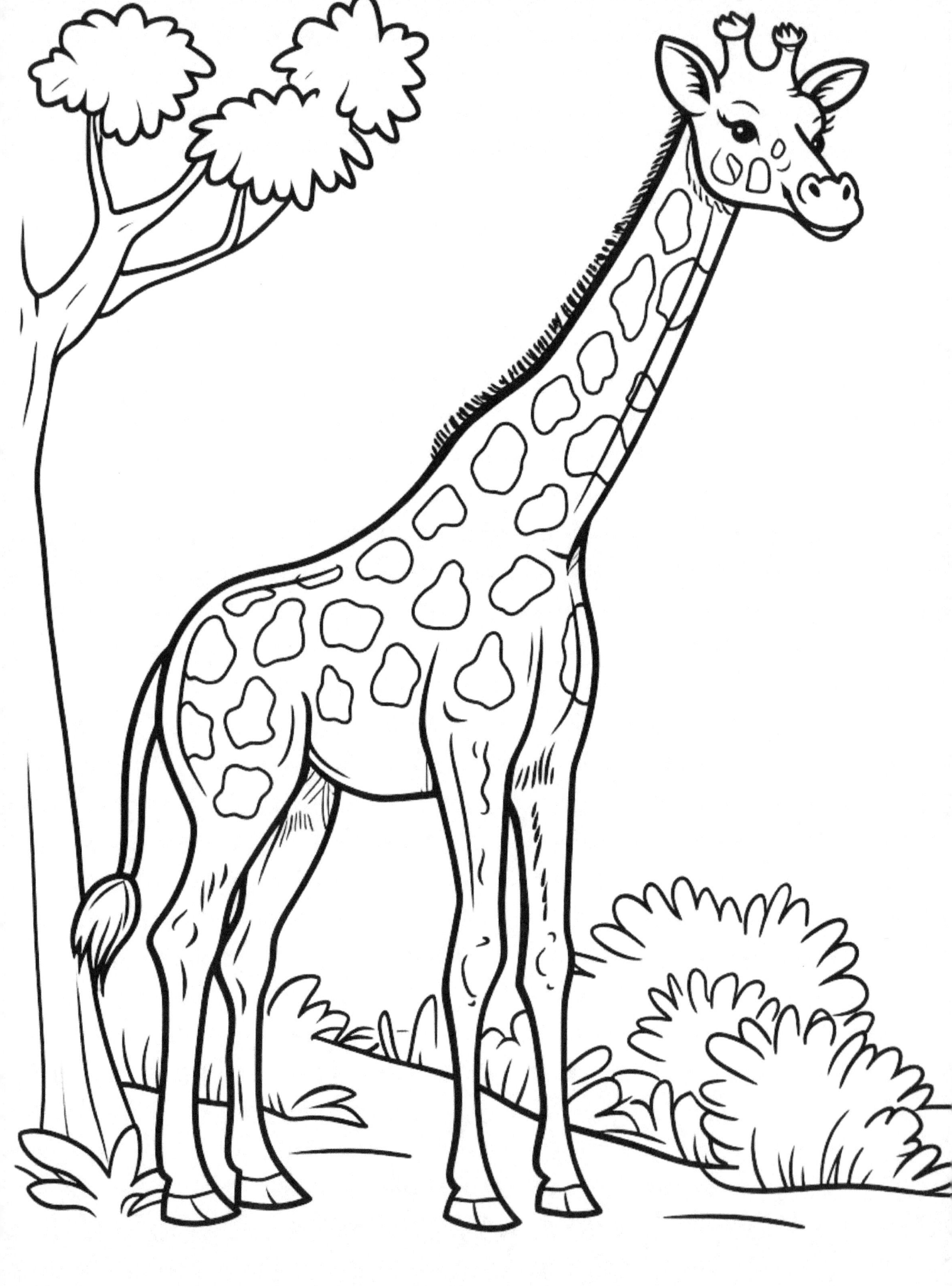

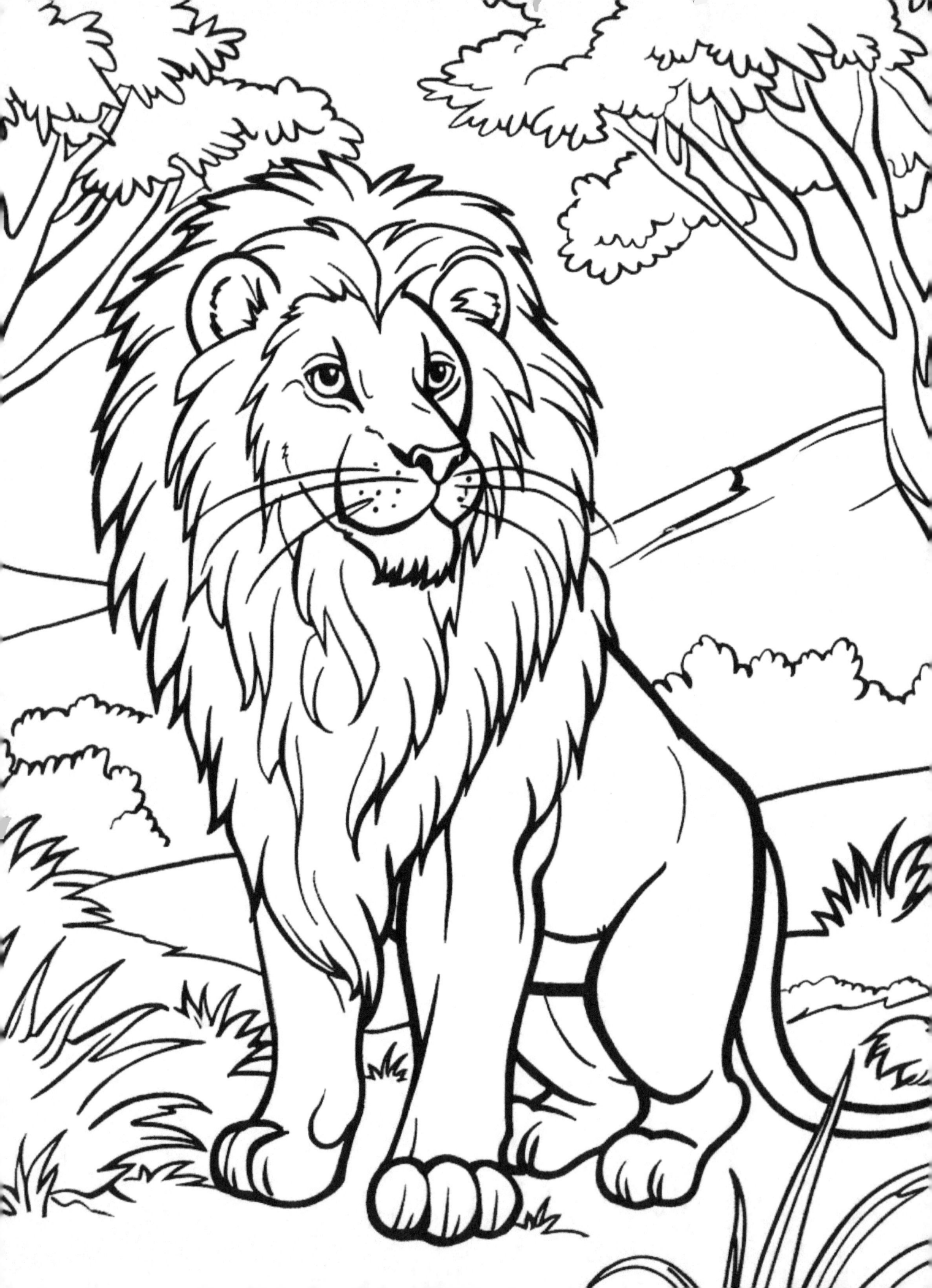

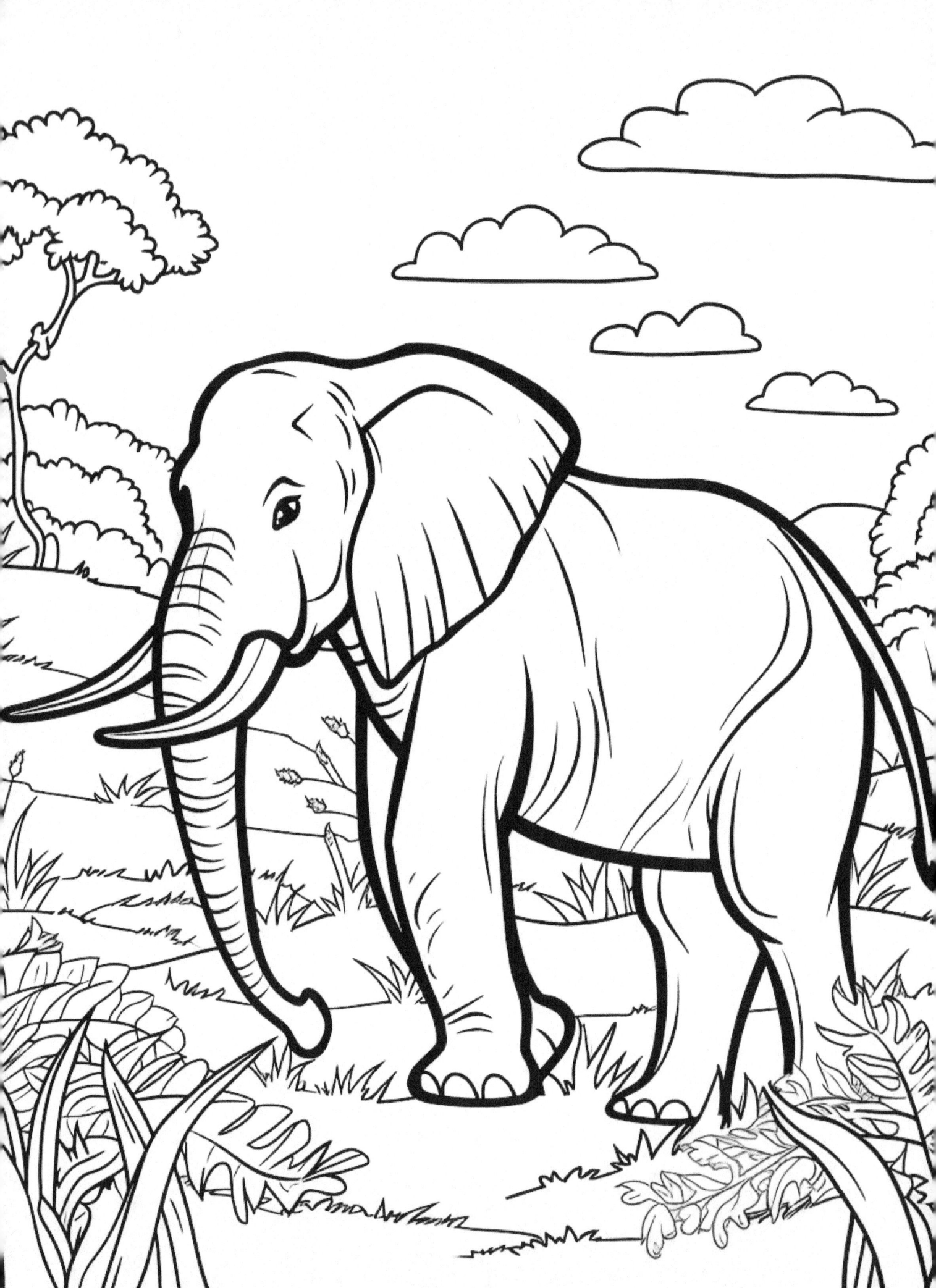

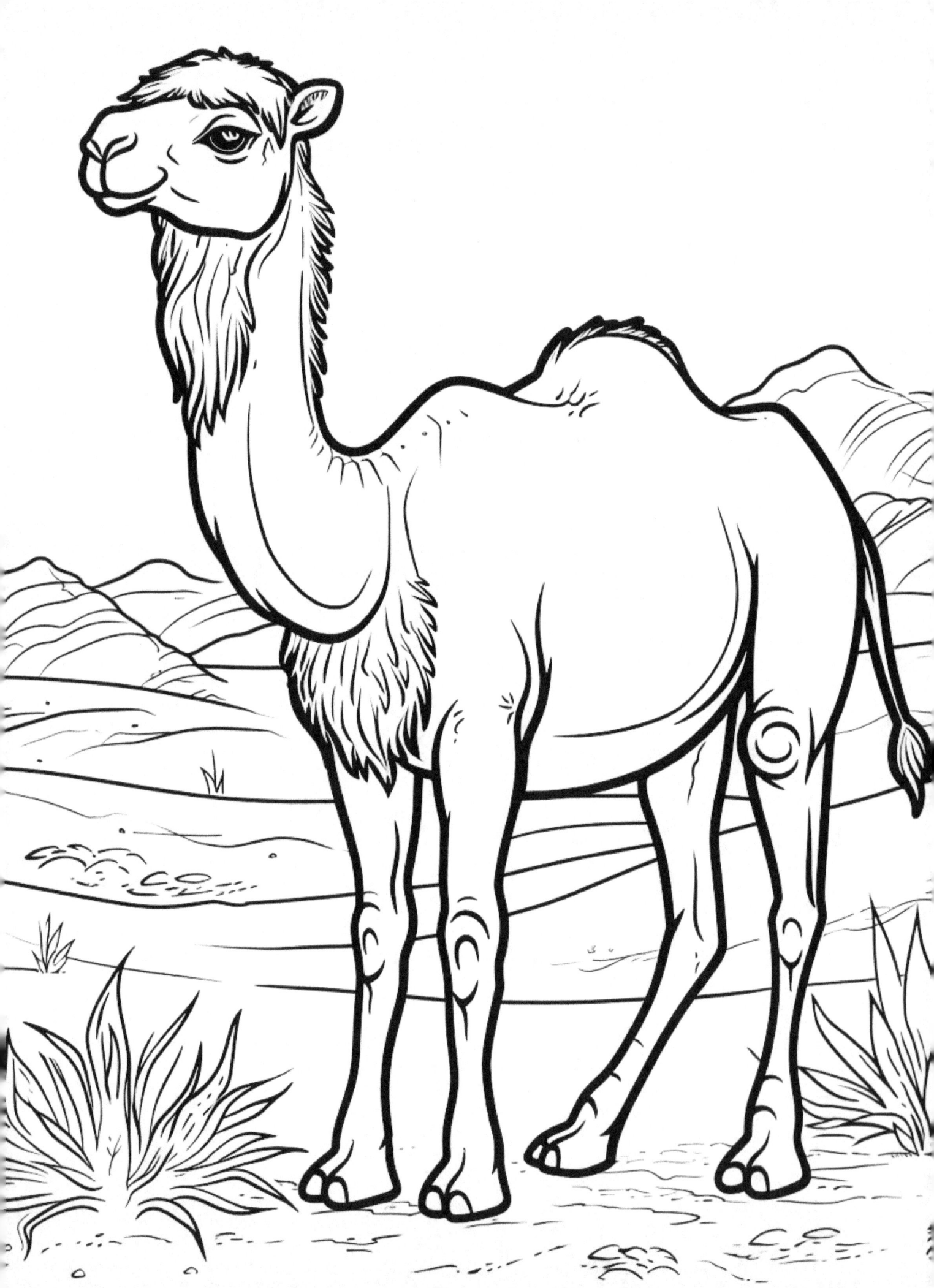

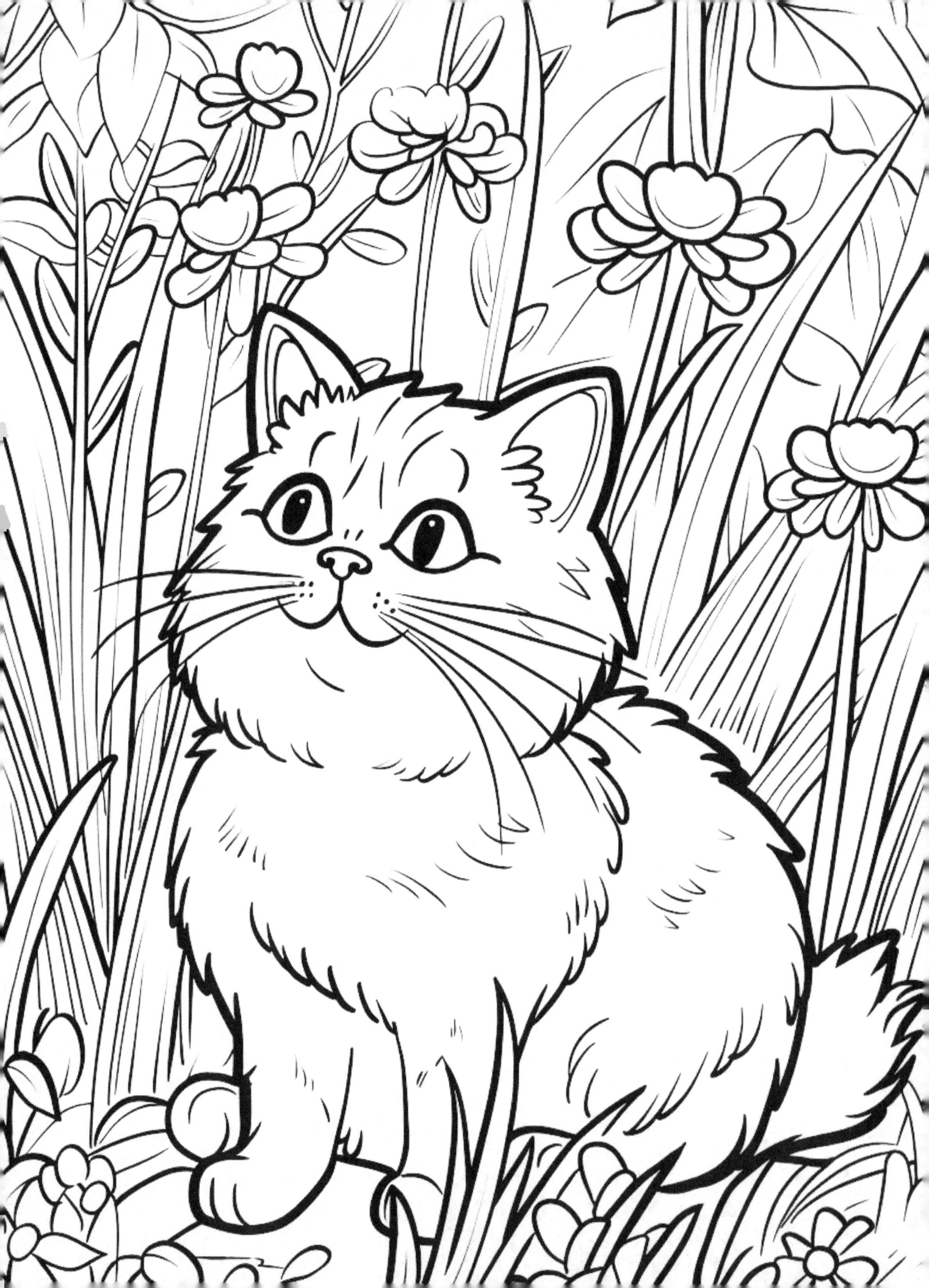

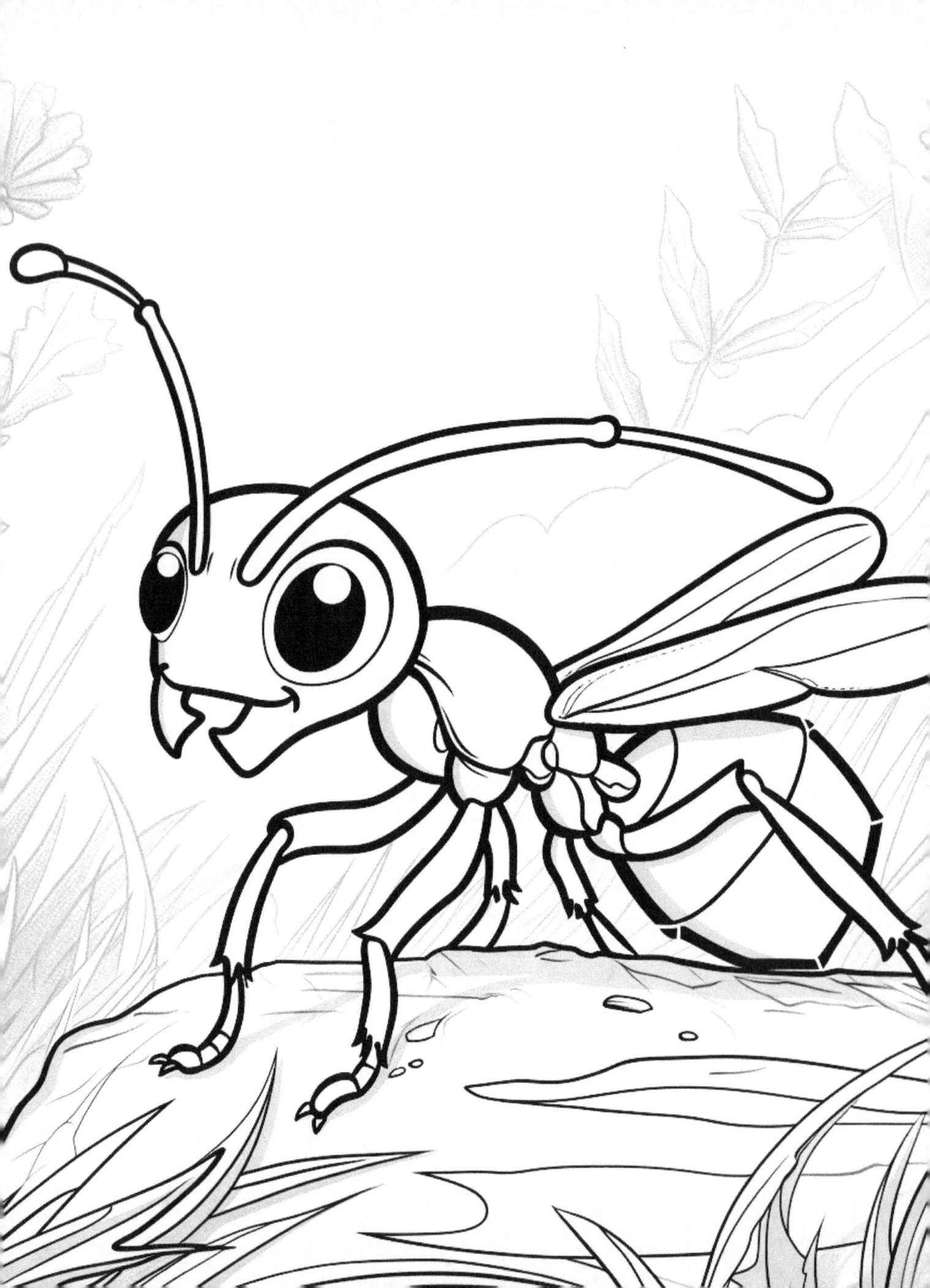

Thank You for Coloring the World!

Your creativity has brought these animals and landscapes to life, filling them with vibrant colors and unique expressions.

I hope you enjoyed this coloring adventure! Remember, the world is full of wonder, just waiting to be explored.

Keep coloring, keep exploring, and keep sharing your artistic spirit!

Share your colorful creations with us! I love to see your masterpieces. Leave a review with your picture on Amazon.

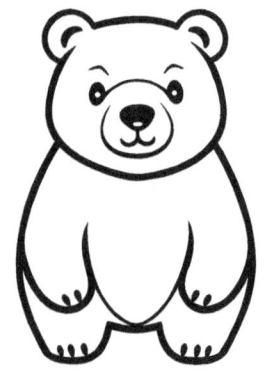

With gratitude,
Artur Sobolevskij

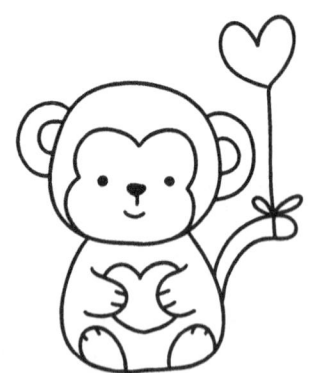